MW01015555

THE

SCOTCHMAN IN AMERICA.

———◇———

ADDRESSES, SONGS, ETC., AT SCOTTISH GATHERINGS; RELIGIOUS
POEMS AND OCCASIONAL VERSES.

———

BY

JOHN PROUDFOOT.

———

CLEVELAND:
FAIRBANKS, BENEDICT & CO., PRINTERS.
1873.

THE SCOTCHMAN IN AMERICA.

ADDRESSES, SONGS, ETC., AT SCOTTISH
GATHERINGS.

SCOTLAND.

ADDRESS TO THE ST. ANDREW'S SOCIETY OF CLEVELAND,
NOVEMBER 30, 1846.

> " From scenes like these old Scotia's grandeur springs,
> That make her lov'd at home, rever'd abroad."
> —BURNS.

DEAR COUNTRYMEN—

In this good enterprise,
One, proud of being a sharer in your joys,
Congratulates your first St. Andrew's Day—
Would for the same he had a worthier lay !

To tender emigrants from Scotia's shore
Aid or advice ; to help a brother poor ;
To cherish " auld acquaintance ; " and to fan
The love of country and the pride of clan,
In vast Columbia, where Lake Erie laves
Ohio's glory with enriching waves,
Hold ye society.   Well this is good—
Worthy " the land of mountain and of flood."

2

Nor does this scheme betray a narrow mind—
A charity too selfish and confined ;
At variance with that universal love,
So plainly taught in precepts from above.
If partial be our charity bestow'd,
'Tis not more so than raising it the mode.
Nor stints it our benevolence the least
In blessing otherwise as seemeth best.
Good-will is shown to all mankind, their due ;
But, to a countryman, affection too.
Not less we love the world, but more our home,
As Brutus, loving Cæsar, more loved Rome.
Here in our day societies are found—
Some called the Grand, and some the Odd abound;
Hallowed with secrets, mystic grip, and sign,
And proud regalia, and badge divine.
But this has got arcana none to bind ;
No word or grip withal to raise the wind ;
Nor is there aught a lurking fear to cause
That slighted are the people, customs, laws.
From Scotland's tut'lar Saint it takes its name,
And with her motto seeks to spread its fame ;
Giving, in hope of nothing back in lieu—
No benefit—no selfish end in view.
Public are all its deeds, and this its chief—
The granting brother countrymen relief.
And, lives there in this world of woods and lakes

One blessed with plenty, from " the land o' cakes,"
That will not, in a natal pride of heart,
Glory in this and take a social part?
Forbid it, Heaven! not for his sake alone—
Scotland 's disgraced by him, a bastard son!
Well may that country he adopts, with reason,
Mark him a fugitive, but fit for treason!
Yes; give me for a citizen the man
Who ne'er forgets his native land or clan;
He who in joy takes warmly by the hand,
Afar from home, one of a father-land.
In such a soul true patriotism glows
And will (live where he may) itself disclose.
Of all the countries on the peopled earth,
From Scotland I would rather claim my birth.
And does American ask, laughing, why?—
Of Britain let him boast as well as I.
His laws—his manners—yea, his sires renown'd
Were hers, and may as such with pride be own'd.
Then let him join us, while on Fancy's wing
Home we revisit and in fondness sing.

Hail! native Caledonia! how grand
From ocean's wave appears thy rugged strand!
And how majestic in the azure skies
Thy purple heath-plumed mountain-tops arise!
Thy ports we enter—large, capacious stores
O'erhang the wharves along the sounding shores!

Huge manufactories rear their heads on high,
With all the thunder of machinery!
Streets lengthen out where Art and Labor toil,
Where Commerce throngs, or Wealth and Fashion smile.
Buildings arise, the work of ages past,
Designed in glory, ever more to last!
From dingy city to the rural scene
Come let us hie; the roads, so smooth and clean,
Invite; and, health inhaling, from the gay
Sunny hill top, the country round survey;
Mark where our fathers dwelt in days of yore,
Or trace the scenes of youth and love once more.
O! what a prospect opens to the sight,
(Unlike, Ohio, thine!) extensive, bright
And varied!   See! behind, range above range,
The mountains rise incult, romantic, strange!
Glaciers, like gems, adorn the lofty steep,
While round their sides stray, numberless, the sheep.
Wrapt in his plaid the shepherd tunes his lute,
His faithful colly in attendance mute.
Before, all shining in the noon-tide beam,
A classic river pours its silver stream.
On either slanting side, and far till lost
In ocean rippling round the shelving coast,
Reigns Agriculture, and in bount'ous smile,
Nature despite, repays her votary's toil.
O'er all the varied landscape scattered, white
Farmsteads and cottages entrance the sight!

In each direction wind the level roads,
And airy bridges span the tumbling floods.
Gay hawthorn hedge encloses many a field
Which yearly doth the crops successive yield ;—
One lies in pasture, where the blackening herd
Feeds, or reposes on the verdant sward.
Another waves in oats, that to the swain,
Whether in cakes or parritch, is the grain.
A third luxuriates with the wheaten sheaf.
A fourth with ryegrass and the clover leaf.
A fifth as fallow, of all weeds to clean.
'Nips and potatoes flourishing in green.
Blithe at his team the plough-boy draws the drill
Straight to the eye, exulting in his skill.
Crows pick behind him ; from the sloethorn bush
Whistle the blackbird and the mellow thrush ;
The jocund cuckoo and the plaintive dove
Alternate hail him from the neighboring grove ;
While over head the laverock soaring high,
With rapt'rous music fills the list'ning sky.

Here, in this wood of aged elms and oaks,
Dark with the wings of congregated rooks,
An ancient castle stands, where chevalier,
In feudal times, undaunted couch'd the spear ;
And titled Beauty lighted up the hall
To minstrelsy and jolly feast and ball.
There, the old abbey rears its Gothic head

Amid the gloom of quiv'ring aspen shade.
In fretted cloister, where the monk austere
Did rigid penance, foxes make their lair;
And where the vestal nun did vigils keep
Wild roses blow and ivy-tendrils creep.
On yonder gentle eminence, half hid
With green plantation peeping through the shade
Appears the graceful villa; pleasure ground
With intersecting flowery walks around.
Fair in the sun and shelter'd from the north
The perfect garden spreads its treasure forth.
'Neath skies of glass the vine in clusters prime
Outvies the best of this her native clime.
In buds and flowers smiles an eternal spring,
While on each spray the birds unceasing sing.
Hurrah! o'er hill and dale and per'lous ground
The sportive yeomen on their chargers bound.
Rous'd from his den the fox excursive wheels,
Th' unkennel'd pack fierce howling at his heels.
Nor floods wild roaring or the quagmire deep;
Nor gaping ditch, high hedge, or craggy steep,
Daunts in the least—all seems an easy path
To top the chase and glorious see the death!
Tallyho! tallyho! with man and horse and hound
The mountains echo and the woods resound.
Adown the glen, where curls like incense sweet
The hamlet's smoke, the parish church we greet.
The heaven-directing spire bids man descry

That happiness lies in yon upper sky.
Hark!—do we hear the Sabbath's chiming bell?
Or is the toll some friend's departing knell?
Thrice hallowed spot!—there did our fathers keep
Assembly solemn, and there now they sleep!
The sculptur'd marble mutely showing forth—
Grateful memorials—their living worth.
Yonder appears, yet young and beautiful,
Our Alma Mater, in the village school.
A haze of doubt permits us not to see
If that the present our Preceptor be;
If yet the benches be the same, and desk
At which we sat and conn'd our hornbook task;
Or if the discipline of leathern taas,
That made us quail, enforces still the laws.
These now we *guess at*—now presume to scan,
So much are we become th' American.
Nor can we trace the scenes of school-boy fun,
Without the thoughts of melancholy dun
Darkening our brow, like April showers the sun—
The foaming waterfall; the limpid burn;
The dizzy cliff; the hoary shapeless cairn;
The flower-enamell'd mead; the heathery fell;
The gowany lea; the clover-scented dell;
The breckany brae; the broomy skirted knowe;
The birken shaw; and fairy haunted howe.
As fancy and the memory bring to view
Those lovely scenes in all their native hue,

Scottish amusements and the manners bland
Before us pass in panorama grand—
The New Year's happy welcome, gift or feast,
With social chat, and song, and harmless jest;
The ardent curlers glorying in their skill,
And roaring play-shots of the famous 'spiel;
The city's shows and corporate concerns;
The country's plowing matches, fairs, and kirns;
The solemn work-pause of the Sabbath day,
Reading at home, if not at church to pray;
Its evening catechising round the fire
And family worship of the reverend sire;
The neighbor younkers met around the hearth,
Holding their halloween or party mirth;
The wedding with its gallop for the brose,
The bride-cake, haggis, and the dance jocose;
The burial, in all its mournful gloom,
Slow moving to the family's ancient tomb.
To mark our birth-place all the soul 's awake,
But 'tis so changed the heart is like to break.
Marred by the hand of time, "sweet home" is there—
The streamlet trotting by; the fountain clear;
The twigs we planted waving high and great;
But where 's the aged elm that graced the gate?
The dog that fawn'd? the arm-chair by the fire?
The dear loved crony? sister? mother? sire?
Alas! no more! and all the scenes of youth
Stript of their charms forever—of a truth!

O Scotland ! were it not but for thy soil,
Sterile and bleak ; thy night and day's hard toil
For scarce a living ; and thy bounds, forsooth
Too circumscrib'd for population's growth,
Few of thy sons would be induced to roam
In quest of riches or a happier home.
'Tis stern necessity that doth compel
Thousands to take of thee the last farewell.
And praised be Heaven that in this western world,
Beneath the flag of Liberty unfurl'd,
A panacea can be found t' assuage
All such complaints, and emigrant engage.
Here, Industry may gain a recompense
And frugal care be crown'd with competence.
Then, while the left behind and " auld lang syne "
Thrill through the soul, come, let us ne'er repine,
But grateful bless the kind directing hand
That led us hither to this goodly land.
In pleasant places hath our lot been cast,
With mercies varied, numberless, and vast.
The land we left still claims our filial tears ;
The land we live in aye our hearty cheers.
But on our better feelings Scotia still
Hath higher claims.   Her scenes and customs fill
The soul with love and veneration ; yet
What prides us most are these her truly great
That stand confest, since Learning's earliest dawn,
The ornaments of science and of man.

In Mathematics and Philosophy,
What names are found of more celebrity
Than Newton's friend, MacLaurin, than Ferguson,
Keill, Gregory, Simpson, he* of Marchistone;
Or Hutcheson, Reid, Stewart, Combe, and Brown?
Unmatched for deep research, and useful truths,
Is not the " Wealth of Nations," Adam Smith's?
For classic elegance and taste refined,
For strict veracity with grace combined,
Say what historian does the past illume
Like Robertson, Buchanan, Smollet, Hume?
Of all the "masters of the healing art"
In foiling Death of his almighty dart
Or blocking up each passage to the tomb,
Is one before an Arbuthnot, a Combe,
A Cullen, Abercrombie, or Munro?
The shade of Esculapius answers, "No!"
For sound Theology and Scripture lore,
For practical religion that is more,
What country ever such divines did own
As Chalmers, Boston, Blair, Dick, Erskine, Brown,
The dauntless Knox, and all that glorious host
Of martyr-worthies of whom Heaven doth boast?
Let Nature's poet, Burns, of humble birth;
Let Scott, the mighty wizard of the north;
Let Thompson, songster of the seasons' strain;

---

* Napier, the discoverer of the Logarithims.

Let Ramsey, chaunter of the past'ral scene;
Let the proud bards of satire, hope, and time;*
The " Voice of Cona,"† mournfully sublime,
With other sons of verse, a numerous throng,
Prove that the Muses' haunt, the land of song,
The scene of heroism, love, romance,
Is Scotland, in a most peculiar sense!
Look where we may, on either side abound
True marks of genius' consecrated ground:
Rivers meander sweet in lyric lays;
Great battle-fields lie crown'd in deathless bays;
Wild woods in story wave in living green;
Auld kirks survive in tales of Fairy Queen; ·
The humble cot, for beauty, love, and truth
Enstamp'd in ethics with immortal youth!
Let the interior of Afric tell
Of traveler Park, and where and how he fell.
And let both poles the sailor Ross declare,
Whose daring soul rear'd Britain's ensign there.
As critic, barrister, and politician,
As moralist, professor, and logician,
Jeffrey, Macaulay, Brougham, Mackenzie, Kaimes,
Wilson, Lees, Chambers, and a thousand names
That in the literary world do shine,
Resplendent suns, are, Modern Athens,‡ thine.
Nor are there lacking monuments to tell

---

* Byron, Campbell, and Pollock.   † Ossian.   ‡ Edinburgh.

That Scotia's sons as artizans excel.
Sculpture and painting, architecture, all
Confess their genius true—original.
Where is the land their music, skill, and taste
Have not delighted, benefited, blest?
The Menai Bridge hangs on their Telford's name;
The locomotive gives their Watts to fame; [claim.*
While the first steamboat is their Taylor's rightful

And is there need to harp of martial glory,
Vast prodigies of valor all their story?
Unconquer'd by the conquerors of this world
Their flag of Freedom hath been aye unfurl'd!
Rome's haughty eagles could not soar beyond
Their Grampian hills, though earth besides she bound.
Since the great Fingal to the present time
Their bravery has been felt in every clime.
Witness the glory of " the bonnet blue "
Upon the ensanguined plains of Waterloo.
There Scotchmen's valor gave the total rout—
" Scotland forever ! " the victorious shout.
Does Spain in her fell Cortez still exult?
France in Napoleon's trophies red with guilt?
Does of his Peter justly vaunt the Russ?
And of his dauntless Tell the hardy Swiss?

---

* The individual who had the distinguished honor of first applying steam power to propel vessels on the water was Mr. James Taylor, tutor in the family of Miller of Dalswinton, Dumfrieshire. See 58th No. of Chambers' Edinburgh Journal.

Do these United States make grateful boast
Of their great Washington, himself a host?
Well—be it so—Scotland, though poor and small,
Can vie in chiefs with each of them and all!
Hers is a Wallace, braver never born!
And hers a Bruce at Freedom's Bannockburn!
And last, though not the least, our rhymes to grace,
Let the Scotch bonnie lassie have a place.
And this essaying, shall we her compare
To those of other lands esteemed as fair?
No; beauty's standard is the lover's brain,
Ideal all, and hence all contrast vain.
But if a form that 's symmetry complete,
Of Nature's perfect moulding, graceful, sweet;
If auburn curls hung o'er the snowy neck;
The blended lily and carnation cheek;
The dewy red-rose lip; the keen blue eye,
Darting the shafts of love, resistless, sly;
If true simplicity, devoid of art;
If blushing modesty; a feeling heart;
A charming voice; a fascinating smile;
A bosom chaste, devout, and without guile;
If prudence, thrift—an economic worth;
Good name, respectability of birth;
A native loveliness without, within—
If these, we say, have any power to win,
Then Jenny's such, and of her sex the queen!

Now, Brother Scot and half-Scot Jonathan,
Come, let us in this country act the man ;
And prove that worthy, every way, are we
Our place of birth and noble pedigree.
May nothing low, dishonest, or unjust
Humble our natal glory in the dust ;
Or show that Scottish blood, by any means,
Degenerate flows in transatlantic veins.
In this our charity let us " go on,"
Nor once draw back while there's a suppliant moan.
To aid the stranger, still the orphan's cry,
And cause the widow's heart to sing for joy,
Are deeds which, of all others, give the best
Reward—the bliss of blessing the distressed.
Let honor, virtue, piety, and peace
Be ever ours, that so our future race,
Proud of their sires, in foreign land may vaunt :
" I am of Scotland and of Scotch descent."

OUR OLD HOME.

READ AT THE ST. ANDREW'S SOCIETY GATHERING, 1848.

Hail Brither Scots! ance mair again
To hold St. Andrew's we convene;
Blythe, hale, and hearty every ane
      On Erie's shore,
Social, to tell the youthfu' scene
      Of days o' yore.

And is not this (without dissembling),
Amidst sic cheer worth while assembling?
To drap ae night the eager scrambling
      For warly pelf,
And, over Scotia's mountains rambling,
      To air aneself?

Ay! then we go! our fare is paid—
The seas are cross'd, just at a stride;
Swifter than telegraphic pride
      Is Fancy's flight;
And now, we 're on the ither side
      And a' is right.

Now come away my neebor Johnnie,
You want to find a youthful cronie,
Wi' wham you 've had splores rare and monie :
    He 's yonder, see!
Now wed to Meg, your sweetheart bonnie,
    Wi' bairnes three.

And Will, I ken what ye are after,
Auld Auntie's gear to mak ye dafter;
Weel—there 's her grave—nae scene o' laughter!
    But blast your luck!
Your cousin Ned, by lawyer craft there,
    'S got every plack!

And come, my worthy Alderman,
In this low cot your life began.
Outside, how neat it looks and gran'!
    Exchange your berth?
Poortith and Care sit dull and wan
    Around the hearth!

Ho, Tam! wi' you I want some fun—
We 'll yet be poachers wi' our gun
When twilight wi' her mantle dun
    Conceals the spot.
Look out! there 's Corbie Jock' la! run!
    Else you 'll be shot.

Dick, come alang; ye want to learn
How shuttles fly and jennies turn;
Gif that the 'factries up the burn
   A han' will take—
Hoolie! my fier, to spin their yarn
    They 've now a strike!

So, Charlie! fain ye want to see
Your puir auld mither wha' o' thee,
Her only boy across the sea,
   Thinks late and early.
Ah dool! you 're tauld when she did dee—
    Her last word, "Charlie!"

Guid, Rab! let 's hae a tramp wi' you man
And seek your Billy, left a yeoman
Wi' gun and dogs. He as a ploughman
   Now croons his sonnet;
And to his dame, a haughty woman!
    Doth doff his bonnet.

Hech me! in this our hameward jaunt,
Can nane amang us happy vaunt:
"I fin' things a' as I do want"?
   'Tis unco this!
But here a pedant looks content,
    Ablins he has.

a

Right learned sir! just look around—
Hill, river, glen, wood, loch, tow'r, mound—
All! all is consecrated ground
    By Genius' fire,
And lives eternal in the sound
    Of Scottish lyre!

O yes, " my rhyme composing Billie,"*
Let 's mount your Pegasus, sae wily,
At ilka well, o'erhung wi' lily,
    We 'll hae a draft;
'Twill mak us like Castalian gillie—
    Poetic daft.

Yonder are mountains, far away;
Their beetling peaks o' granite gray;
Around their sides at break o' day
    The mist rolls dreary;
While at their feet the lambkins play
    In frolic merry.

As chieftains now we tread together
A waste o' purple blooming heather,
Our very souls hae snapt the tether
    O' human frame!
And pure ethereal—thither—hither
    Exults at hame!

---

* Burns.

Out frae our path wee pousie springs;
The patrick whirrs; the muir cock dings;
Aboon our head the laverock sings,
   And plover whistles;
While peesweep flap wi' gladsome wings
   The down o' thistles.

And now we 're on sweet gowany braes
Down which the burnie gurg'ling plays;
Aroun', the kye and stirkies graze
   In peacefu' mood,
Or fu', reclining at their ease,
   They chew their cud.

Next, in the lovely strath we roam—
Thro' birken-shaw; thro' yellow broom;
Thro' meads of variegated bloom,
   Where hum of bees,
Gay butterflies, and sweet perfume
   The senses please.

Anon, we mark the village scene—
The schule; the kirk; the mill between;
The hawthorn gray; the holly green;
   The crystal well
Where lads and lassies meet at e'en
   Their loves to tell.

Whist! now we 're in the fairy dell,
Where ghaists and witches scream and yell!
We 'll cross the stran', and—Wow! the spell,
      Waesucks! is broken.
And now of ither things we tell
      Than the last spoken.

See! here a puir o'erlabor'd wretch
Digs for a living in a ditch;
Tho' honest, yet scorned by the rich
      And haughty 'squires;
And there, in russet, a sweet witch
      Is muckin' byres!

The gaberlunzie, hat in han',
Sits on the Brig,—"a puir blin' man!"
While Elspie, hirp'ling as she can
      Half clad in rags,
At every door, there, takes her stan'
      Wi' mealy bags!

Eneugh! eneugh! eneugh we 've seen,
Let us to Cleveland back again;
What tho' Cuyahoga lacks the sheen
      Of Scotia's river;—
And scenes monotonous, I ween,
      Be like Hers—never;

Yet such have something mair to give,
Can teach us, "independent live!"
And mak us, gif we 're eydant, thrive
      Nor know what want is!
Can—'till our kytes are like to rive
      Feast us on dainties!

Then in your patriotic zeal,
Forego of Scotia the ideal,
And gratefu' here enjoy the real,
      As doth become ye a';
A credit to the common-weal
      O' great Columbia!

Come! let us toast this happy night
Together, in a bumper bright,
The land we left, our dear delight,
      And this we live in!
Nae country 's like them bravely right
      Under wide heaven!

JULY THE FOURTH.

READ AT A St. Andrew's Festival in response to the Toast,
"The Fourth of July."

Let ither bards, a venal gang,
   At Levee celebration,
In fulsome flatt'ry raise a song
   To coofs o' royal station;
I touch the lyre, uncouthly strung,
   For fun and recreation,
To Freedom's day as held amang
   The folks o' Yankee nation—
          A glorious day !

At previous Anniversary Feast
   Of Scotland's great Apostle,
We 've sung—(or tried to sing at least)
   Her bonny scenes and thistle,
Now Jonathan and Buckeye crest—
   The land in which we bustle,
Deserves a stanza o' the best,
   A blast upon our whistle
          To trump his day.

Soon as the hour of midnight rings
    Gay, frae the city steeple—
Lang ere the dawn her saffron flings
    O'er woods of sugar maple—
In thunder note the cannon sings,
    Bells chime frae ilka chapel,
While roosters roused clap their wings,
    An' craw'd, "Gude save the people,
              The Fourth to-day!"

Anither and anither roar
    Come louder yet and louder!
Sleep flies affrighten'd in his snore
    Thro' winnocks smashed wi' powder,
And hark! the train-bands in a tour
    Play "Yankee Doodle" prouder
Than when their sires, in days of yore,
    Set shou'der firm to shou'der
              And gain'd the day.

And now to meet the noble fun
    The boys are out to jump it;
The gilpey gals in twilight dun
    Are also fix't to romp it;
While thro' the town afore the sun
    Mechanics' hammers thump it,
Rearing proud arches many a one,
    And banners star-strip'd stampit
              To grace the day.

To join the city's public mirth
   The farmers roun' declare it;
Sae teams and buggies south and north
   Come ratt'ling in to share it;
E'en auld guid wives and young go forth,
   And sons and daughters dare it.
Wha wadna' on the glorious Fourth
   Show independent spirit
          And bliss THE day?

The auspicious, look'd for, welcome morn
   In beauty shone the dearest;
Summer the forest did adorn
   In robes of green the fairest;
A rainbow span'd the meadows shorn,
   And rivers flow'd the clearest;
While Plenty strew'd, from out her horn,
   Each path with fruit the rarest
          To crown the day.

Over his varied gamut ran
   The wood-fledged actor,* laughin';
The humming-bird in flowery lawn
   The nectar dews was quaffin';
In sunny glade the sportive fawn
   And squirrel droll were daffin;
All nature seemed to join wi' man,
   And sharer be a half in
          His joys that day.

---

* The mocking-bird.

See! on the green beneath the shade
  The crowd promiscuous gathers,
To form the lengthened gran' parade
  Of firemen, troops, and ithers;
The country's worthies at their head
  And city's sapient fathers.
Give way!—now moves the cavalcade
  Harmonious, all like brithers
          Meet sic a day.

Along this street and that in sheen
  They march in file before ye,
Wi' music's patriotic strain,
  And flags display'd in glory;
While, hailing the triumphal scene
  From palm-ornated story,
Loved beauty and the veteran
  Of Seventy-six, now hoary,
          Are seen that day.

Anon they halt where they did start
  And, at the word commanded,
Are by artillery's report
  And hearty cheers disbanded.
Let hostile powers learn frae this sport
  If on our coast they landed
Heroes are ready to retort
  In millions when demanded,
          Just ony day.

But come! and let us to the Kirk
   Where crowds on crowds assemble;
We fain would ken this day their wark
   And gif they don't dissemble;
Mess John wi' ithers o' the ark
   With fervent prayer preamble,
Recites THE DECLARATION stark,
   As Jotham did his bramble
          To friends ae day.

All right—nae doubt to fan the spark
   (If waning,) patriotic—
To fire at crowns—a royal mark!—
   Your cannon democratic.
But (please your reverences) hark!
   To brand wi' curse emphatic
My father 'cause he drew the dirk
   'Gainst yours once, is not attic
          'Fore me this day.

"Verbum sat sapienti."   Jove!
   Now for our theme come nerve us,
In yonder amaranthine grove
   Celestial scenes deserve us;
Scenes on which angels from above
   Look down and fain would serve us—
The SUNDAY SCHOOLS convened in love,
   Asking, "What means this service?"
          Of sires this day.

O, what a lovely shining throng
  Of infant souls before us!
The pæan swells from lisping tongue,
  And parents join the chorus,
The Plymouth Rock begins the song
  " What Goodness hath done for us."
Floods, lakes, and woods the notes prolong,
  And Heaven's high arch encore us,
         Well pleased this day.

Engaged in this delightful scheme
  We find the pious preacher;
And greatly glorious in the same
  The sage laborious teacher;
If aught on earth can merit Fame,
  Or up to Heaven reach her,
It is the patriotic aim
  Of making Youth the voucher
         Of Truth some day.

Yes, to transmit, pure and entire,
  To rising generation
The boon of Revolution sire,
  Give pious education;
Then in the scale of empire higher
  Shall rise our much-loved nation;
Justice around her, walls of fire,
  And the Arts her proud munition
         To latest day.

But hark ! these seraph bands dismiss
With benediction solemn :
" God of our Pilgrim Fathers, bliss
   Our offspring, and enrol 'em
All, as thy own peculiar race
   In Heaven's eternal volume,
That, for a witness o' thy grace,
   There may a living column
             Be found each day."

Now post meridian smiles the sun,
   Down frae the cloudless carry,
As if in Freedom's gratefu' fun
   He wanted to be mirry ;
While, ere this day of days be done,
   Some wi' their charmin' dearie
On steamer trip or railway run
   Go off hurrain' cheerie,
             Fu' blythe that day.

Others again met wi' some friend
   Or youthfu' bosom crony,
'Round festive board the glad hours spend
   In tales and speeches mony ;
Of wit and toast there is no end,
   And sentiment how bonny !
If Kings and Queens the ha'f but kenn'd
   They 'd doff their crowns to Jonnie
            And hail his day.

Nor less, the freed school-boy enjoys
   This day renowned in story;
On public grounds he lifts his voice
   And sweats in sportive hurry;
The squib and cracker's bursting noise
   The stranger collie worry;
The grand display of novel toys
   A harvest is of glory
          To him that day.

The athletic youths are also seen
   In dextrous feat contending
'Mid circling crowds upon the green,
   And plaudit shouts ascending.
Here farmers frae the "rural scene,"
   The year's first fruits are vending,
And there the pedlar spreads in sheen
   His notions rare, commending
          Wi' puff that day.

Nor ends with night this gala joy,
   It wi' the dark increases;
Tar-barrels piled up mountain high
   A bane-fire brightly bleezes;
And winnocks lit up all forby
   Beam forth ten thousand graces,
Which are reflected gloriously
   On happy smiling faces,
          En masse that night.

And when the beacon flames get low
   And candles burn the socket,
Lo ! Pyrotechny takes the show
   And fires his wondrous rocket.
Wi' streaming whizz some upwards go,
   Bright meteors, strange to look at ;
Others, like fiery serpents, thro'
    The startling crowd scouts crockit—
          Rare sport that night. .

Like circular saw, one buzzing turns
   Unto yon post attached ;
Along the line another burns
   In mottoes bright unmatched ;
And see ! the fired balloon now spurns
   The ground to be detached—
Anon it mounts up to the starns,
   Wi' the day's news despatched
          That very night.

But it would take a' July the Fourth,
   To gie a bare rehearsal
Of one tenth o' the public mirth—
   Rejoicings universal.
Nor wonder if this theme of worth
   Be marr'd by Scottish verse ill ;
'T would take a bard of Yankee birth,
   Wi' numbers quaint and terse all,
          To tell 't this night.

While forests grow and rivers flow,
  In party or opinion
May there be never aught to sever
  The blessing—blessed UNION;
But may it be from sea to sea
  Extended in dominion,
Till every soul from pole to pole,
  Freedom's devoted minion,
         Hails this its day,

ADDRESS TO THE HIGHLAND BAGPIPES.

READ BEFORE THE ST. ANDREW'S SOCIETY.

Hail, Highland pipes! Scotch a' together!
The glory of the land o' heather!
In days of yore, our chieftain father
               Ye roused to wars.
Now not for strife, but peace, we gather,
                 Let 's bliss our stars!

To stranger ear thy chanter note
And chord of drones may seem Quixote;
But heard as down the strath they float
               On evening's breeze,
Of music sweeter there is naught
                The ear to please.

When play'd wi' Celtic skill and fire
Thy charms surpass the Orphean lyre,
And objects dead wi' life inspire,
               While scenes domestic—
Real Scottish manners, sports, attire—
                All shine majestic!

Some instruments may wake the dance,
And smack of German, Spain, and France;
But common—tame—they can 't|entrance
            Like thee a Scot:
His verra saul he feels at once
            To be thy note!

Oh! what associations fill
His mem'ry at thy warblings shrill!
Auld Caledonia—glen and hill,
            Cascade and river,
Sacred to youth and freedom, still
            Live fresh forever!

Thy crunluath strains in festive hall
Grace love's and beauty's merry ball;
While, mournfu' following the pall
            Of Chieftain gone,
Thy coronach makes tears to fall
            At " the gray stone!"

But chief, upon the embattled field
Thy pibroch peals heroic, wild:
Then midst the clash of sword and shield
            Is heard thy strain;
All other drown'd or forced to yield,
            Laid wi' the slain!

4

At the first Advent, it is said,
The shepherds on the bagpipes played;
Ay! and the angelic serenade
               Was by the same.
Then let all reverence be paid
               To thy great name.

Let not the sanctimonious sot
Condemn the music of the Scot;
Our Temple organ's solemn note
               By such was given;
The bagpipes are, for aught we wot,
               The strains of heaven!

TO THE SCOTCH THISTLE.

READ AT THE ST. ANDREW'S SOCIETY FESTIVAL, 1851.

Hail royal flower! auld Scotia's Thistle!
It does ane good to see your bristle
Sae far frae hame, 'mang Yankee teasel
          Stand up erect.
Wow! to thy praise my rustic whistle
          Sall hae a strike.

There 's mony a sweet and stately flower
Adorns the blooming wild and bower—
The foxglove, lily, and a score
          Of roseate leaf;
But thou 'rt of all the flowery corps
          Enstamp'd the chief.

Aboon them a' thou shoot'st thy stem,
And spreadst thy leaves of spiry hem,
While every blossom, every gem
          Of purple blow,
Shines like a costly diadem
          On monarch's brow.

When in thy summer's bloom array'd,
The butterflies choose in their pride
To sit on thee wi' wings spread wide;
> And bees for honey
Buzz busy on thy ilka side,
> Each blink that 's sunny.

As if Dame Nature's darling care,
On downy pinions light as air
Sown is thy seed—and pristine fair
> O'er mony lands,
(The pride of Flora, rich and rare,)
> Thy bloom expands.

In yellow glory on the fell
The broom and breckan lo'e to dwell,
In native grace o'er haugh and dell
> The gowans glent;
And bonnily the heather bell
> Blooms on the bent.

Yet taken frae their natal sward
Hamesick they die, nor will be rear'd,
Whilst thou shoot'st up thy healthy beard
> Each Scot attendant,
Where'er he owns a Yankee yard
> And 's independent.

Ten hundred years have come and gane
Sin' great Achius beat the Dane,
And bade thee ever bloom the sign
    On Scotland's 'scutcheon,
With " Nane provokes me without pain
    Of due correction."*

Bright symbol of our much loved land !
Beneath thy auspices sae bland,
Happy we feel on Erie's strand
    At annual feast.
St. Andrew ! on us here command
    Thy blessings best !

And for the honor of thy name
And this our Thistle's honest fame,
May it be every Scotchman's aim
    To go it straight ;
Then should he wander far frae hame,
    He 'll aye be richt.

Dear symbol o' my native land,
Still mine upon a foreign strand ;
Significant, expressive, grand
    Thou 'lt bristling wave
Ever, as frae a mither's hand,
    Fresh o'er my grave.

---

* " Nemo me impune lacessit."

REPORT OF THE ST. ANDREW'S SOCIETY
FOR 1852.

———

" Let charity forgive me a mistake,
That zeal, not vanity, has chanced to make ;
And spare the Poet for his subject's sake."
—COWPER.

'Tis now the seventh year since first began
Our movements in this philanthropic plan,
The end of which, to all alike well known,
Would here be needless to descant upon ;
To lend that aid a countryman implores
When landing on these distant stranger shores ;
Or give a Scotchman opportune relief,
Who pines in indigence or sighs in grief.
How far this end may have by stinted means
Accomplished been, reported fact contains ;
And as the cases—alter but the name—
And the narration 's the repeated same,
Let last year's statement of itself suffice
As a synopsis of our charities ;
Yet be it understood, not pharisaic
Trump we our alms, but speak in rhyme-prosaic
Of privileges high on us bestowed—
The bliss of giving—means of doing good.

Love, peace and harmony from first to last
Have reign'd and bound in social ties more fast.
True, difference of opinion there has been
On the best modes to meet the grand design ;
But such, instead of hurting, only tends
T' advance the cause, and swell the list of friends :
So tides and tempests agitate the sea,
And, healthy, from stagnation keep it free.

And first, before the festive glee is gone
Of Christmas, hear ! Friend Janet makes her moan :
" My gude man 's sick—and helpless bairnies four—
Cauld ! cauld 's our hearth—starvation at the door—
Thro' chinky walls—Oh ! come behold our woe !—
Half-dead, and wrapt in winding sheets of snow !—
Ah ! little dreamed I, when at home, I smiled
Midst peace and plenty, a fond mither's child,
That thus to beg I e'er should be compelled !"
   A visit 's paid—the gude man's health returned,
And comfort cheers where want and sorrow mourned.

Nor does the labor of the Board here rest,
To find distress they nobly go in quest
And many a one receives a timely aid,
Averse (tho' grateful) in their native pride.
For with a Scot true born, it is, in brief,
The last alternative to seek relief.

But as in coin there 's counterfeited worth,
So in the world are Scots of spurious birth,
Alloyed with vice, who aimless, idly rove,
As the next applicants too sadly prove :
" I 'm gaun out west to meet in Illinois
A brither there, our name is Mickleroy.
Thus far I 've gat, but a' my cash is done—
An empty pouch to travil wi' 's nae fun.
Gie but five dollars, sae you'll most oblige,
And to remit it soon, my truth I pledge."
He gets the sum, shakes hands and bids good-bye,
But back next day appears Sir Mickleroy,
Demanding more ; and what my friends d' ye think ?
Whitelaw said no ! and why ? he smelled of drink.
Instead of going straight into the car
He paid his passage at yon doggery-bar !
While generous Whitelaw, duped thus bad enough,
Is censured with a charitable laugh.
Well—a divine says somewhere, " Better serve
A drone, a wasp, than let a worker starve." *
And charity, tho' oft' misused, fails never,
Believing all, nor thinking evil ever." †

But who comes next ? he looks both stout and hale,
Does he want alms ? let 's listen to his tale :
" Sir, up this street I met a Scotchman brither,
Wha very kindly did direct me hither,
That frae your funds I might receive a sum

---

* Matthew Henry.   † Paul.

To take me o'er to Canada my home;
A bite o' breakfast I 've not had to-day
And trouth! I 'll starve should I not get away."
On short interrogation he was found
Tekel upon St. Andrew's scales and ground,
And is informed, that he, and such as he,
Had claims not one on the society.
" Yet stop," says Hunter, hospitably shrewd,
" Gie to my house and saw a cord of wood;
And if ye deem that labor rather hard,
I 've got a spade and ye shall delve my yard;
When with the honest earnings you'll get hame.
Do this, or on yoursel' be a' the blame.
Yet here 's out o' my private purse a quarter
For breakfast, nor think ye hae catch'd a Tartar,
But back return to your obliging brither
Wha sent ye here, and get frae him anither;
He weel may spare it—not a single groat
Lends he our funds to help a brither Scot."
    At this he slunk away, but not to dig—
He found it easier, not ashamed, to beg.

    Rather than censure, would I lavish praise
Upon my countrymen and on their ways;
But then, to reprobate such fellows mean
And deeds ignoble, say, who could refrain?
Nor better they, who having wealth to spend
Lack the good will a brother to befriend;

Ay, send him to St. Andrew's for his dole
In all their selfish narrowness of soul.

   Down yon back alley stands the sombre hearse
And a small group with woe come to converse—
Poor Jean is dead! her history soon is told:
Some years ago she left her native fold,
Wed an inebriate who died thro' drink,
Herself and children to the very brink
Of misery brought.   The needle hard she plied
Lost comfort to recall, in honest pride,
But all in vain.   Her health and strength decayed,
Despite our care and kind physician's aid
She breathed her last, commending to her God
Her helpless ones around her weeping loud.
Poor Jean is dead!—and who attends her bier?
Our pious Chaplain with his words of cheer;
While mourner chief, in unaffected woe,
Stands with the orphans, Anderson, our jo!

   But who is this comes leaning on his crutch?
Poor fellow! be he Yankee, Dutch, or Scotch.
"Gude bliss ye, sirs!" he queerly made his plaint,
"I'm by the mither's side of Scotch descent,
But the misfortune had—had to be born—
At all—to lead a roving life forlorn.
On this terraqueous globe there's scarce a port
But I have seen and met with woe and sport.
With five sheets in the wind I've rode it glorious,

And colors hoisted in the fight victorious,
Braved every hardship, danger dared, and death
Laughing defied, and all devoid of scath,
Till on these waters 't was my lot accurst—
Gude save your honors!—whiz!—the boiler burst!
On hauling up, I found on the wharf's shelf
That I was minus some parts of myself,
Lost in this fray, my guarantee to beg—
This is a counterfeit—my cork-wood leg!"

   Go it ye cripple! here's a dollar for ye;
You merit more—were it but for your story.
With this he stumps away in all the joy
And independence of a sailor boy!

   Our worthy President not long ago,
Sat in his office, rocking to and fro,
In thought, no doubt, how to befriend the poor,
When hark! a well-bred tap salutes the door.
Opened—before him strutted cap a-pie,
A gentleman as fine as fine could be!
" Good day." " Good day, sir." " Won't you just walk
    in."
"Thank you," "A chair," "O thank you, Sir," again.
*   *   *   *   *   *   *   *   *
This call was for a draft upon our coffer,
To get him cordial wines—the spendthrift loafer!
Brought up to dress at mirrors—drink with lairds—
Follow the hounds—shoot grouse—and play at cards,

His patrimony he away had fooled ;
And being in no kind of business schooled
Wherewith to mend himself, hit on the plan
Of acting thus the beggar-gentleman.
The doctor gave him some stray pocket-cash
To get him off—avoiding farther fash ;
And as he shut the door was heard to say,
Or rather in a fervent tone to pray :
" Of all the gipsy beggars lank and vile,
Ragged and ruffled that our doors assail,
Preserve us all from the accomplished rake
And prodigal, for charity's dear sake !"

While navigation raises steam and sail,
From immigrant each week brings an appeal.
Of many cases only one we state,
'T will serve our purpose—long reports we hate.
One Monday morning, lands upon our shore
A Scottish family of half a score.
At eastern port they settled had their fare,
To place of destination, west somewhere.
But here their passport further ceased to tell—
The cause some swindler agents knew full well,
As likewise did our noted friend Squire Parks,
Whose law-harpoon soon struck the harbor-sharks.
See ! on the beach this little stranger band,
Confused amid confusion, greets the land.
The honored sire, nonplussed, without a friend,
Each shilling spent, far from his journey's end ;—

The worthy matron, caused by grief of mind
Or tedious passage, lies too soon confined ;
Young Jennie, woman grown, attendant weeps ;—
As on a trunk wee Tommie soundly sleeps,—
Watched by an elder sister, who with care,
The hours beguiling, combs Jemima's hair ;
Whining and hungry Sandy eats a crumb ;—
While Will and Jock back o'er the tide look dumb,
In thoughts away to childhood's happy scenes
Of broomy knowes, sweet burns, and primrose glens.
    And was it all for this you toiled for years ?
Sold at a discount vast your household wares—
The venerable relics, handed down
Thro' line of ancestry of high renown,
To raise as much as would transplant you here,
In hopes to better future days and cheer ?

    Ah ! little think the sordid souls of earth—
The pleasure-jaunting rioters of mirth—
Or even you, ye wealthy merchantmen
Who strut our wharves intent on making gain,
What hardship, care, anxiety, and want
Betide the hapless, houseless immigrant !
Heedless he's passed by, and his little all
Of luggage, miserably poor and small !
Yet dry your tears, dear countrymen, look gay !
The darkest hour 's before the break of day.
See ! Craig and Shanks apprised now of your grief,
Wing'd with compassion, come to your relief.

Your case is weighed—all meet' provision made—
Again you're off—nor winds, nor fears a-head!
And, settled down—all right—you write to Shanks,
Who, self-approving, reads of blessing and of thanks.

At the late fire whose fell devouring flames
Reduced to ashes several happy hames,
Leaving the inmates destitute and poor,
Prompt was assistance—would it had been more!
But yet that little may in such a plight
Crush'd hope inspire thro' life's disastrous fight—
Help crown the future with far brighter days
And Phœnix like, anew from ashes raise.

That Charlie's met by accident his death
Comes on the whisper of compassion's breath.
To his "long home," in absence of his friends,
His countryman, in duty bound, attends.
So brief among us was his sojourn few
His name, his lineage, or his country knew;
Yet still enough our sympathies to claim
And give him burial in St. Andrew's name.
Peace to the stranger! tho' no mother's cares
Soothe his departure; tho' no sister's tears
Bedew his bier; tho' his own parish bell,
Oft heard in infancy, tolls not his knell;
Nor in the grave his father lays his head,
Yet all his obsequies are duly paid.
Peace to the stranger! he as soundly sleeps

Where, with heaven's tears bedewed, the willow weeps,
As if he in his native kirk-yard lay,
Commingling peacefully with kindred clay.

   In the last stage of fell consumption pined,
Under the roof of his employer kind,
Young Stewart, once the sprightly and the glad,
But now, alas! the pensive and the sad.
Of no mean parentage, born where the Clyde
Doth to the sea's embrace meand'ring glide
He spent his youth, yet early left his hame
To see the land of Washington and fame.
A brave good fellow, but improvident,
Misfortune dogged his path where'er he went.
Thro' Mexican campaign dread flashed his brand,
Fighting the foe of his adopted land.
Among the first was he to scale the walls,
And plant the stars o'er Montezuma's halls.
And all for what?—a conqueror to return
With ruined health!—the ashes of the urn!
His plaint how touching!—nothing of renown!
Enough to move the hardest heart of stone!
"Like bird ensnared, and fluttering to be free,
Come death and end my life of misery!
I'll write my mother—no!—'t will break her heart;
In me, her boy, is wrapt her dearest part.
I am a burthen to these stranger friends,
Their kindness kills—no means to make amends—
O! were I in the asylum, where were healed

My wounds received in the ensanguined field,
There would I rest on Charity's made bed
And close mine eyes with the forgotten dead."
    St. Andrew heard the last part of his prayer,
And led his sons to pay his passage there.

    In search of business or in quest of work,
Both able men and willing for a daurk,
Some with a family and some without,
Have made, and seldom made in vain, their suit.
If no employment at the first was found
Their board was paid for till they look'd around
And met it meritorious; some of whom
To show their gratitude have since become
Sons of St. Andrew—anxious to bestow
That aid to others we to them did show.

    Thus case on case might we enumerate,
Varied in circumstance, yet like in weight,
Did time or ev'n necessity give law;
So we conclude with an *et cetera.*

SCOTLAND REVISITED.

READ AT A ST. ANDREW'S FESTIVAL.

Yestreen, ere I gied, sir, away to my bed,
  I sat myself down to think
What I might present this night to our Saint,
  In the way of some homely clink.

Not long while I mused, until that I dozed,
  And, sleeping or waking, did dream,
That you, sir, and self, each astride on an elf,
  Thro' the land of our fathers did skim.

Our feelings were strange, as we witnessed the change
  A few years of absence had wrought.
To receive us, another than sister and mother
  Op'd the door of our father's lov'd cot.

We straitened the girth at the spot of our birth,
  And lingered awhile to survey
The green in the wildwood, where oft we in childhood,
  Barefooted, light-hearted, did play.

5

At the foot o' the yard, on the green grassy sward,
   The lasses were tramping the claes,
While the shepherd, at large, led his white fleecy charge
   Up the moorlan's and heathery braes.

There purled the burn in its whimpling turn,
   And thund'ring leapt over the linn,
Till escaped from the glade, down the gay flow'ry mead,
   It reflected the sun in his sheen.

And there were the huts, and the cleughs, and the grots
   Once the staunch Covenanter's abode,
And there were the fields and the proud Alpin wilds,
   Where Wallace and Bruce dauntless trod!

The glen waved with posies of wild flowers and roses,
   And echoed the sweet warbled strain;
While the gowk wi' the tittlin', still changing their sittin',
   Flew with us athwart the gay scene.

Fam'd mosses and mountains, lochs, rivers, and fountains
   Careering and veering we cross'd,
The auld haunted biggins, sans winnocks and riggins,
   Anon and forever we passed.

At the mouth of a cave washed by the sea wave,
   Me-thought we alighted at last—
With caution we entered, when lo! as we sauntered,
   Before us St. Andrew passed.

He lean'd on a cross, deep transfixed in the moss,
   And seemed to await our address;
His hair, thin and gray, o'er his shoulders did stray,
   And benevolence beamed from his face.

"As pilgrims we come from afar to thy tomb,
   Our filial affection to prove,"—
We daringly said; when the Saint raised his head
   And bespoke us in accents of love:

"Dear children! to honor the thistle-flowered banner,
   Or that of the star-spangled blue,
Give Freedom and Truth an Advocate's mouth,
   And if needed the sword that is true.

"With alms deeds remember the last of November,
   As such is the poor Scotchman's claim."
More than this had he spoke, if I had not awoke—
   And behold! it was all, sir, a dream.

INSTALLATION ADDRESS.

Sirs, at our last meeting,
In hopes of this greeting,
Was I your Installer appointed,
Ye favored elect,
Then attend with respect,
And be each to your office anointed.

PRESIDENT.

And first in the name
Of our Saint, I proclaim
You, sir, fill the chair in divan.
Your duty 's to state
When and where we 're to meet,
Sound the tocsin, and lead in the van,
Money-orders endorse,
Best order enforce,
In everything act out the man.
And, sir, at our hand
You 're presented this brand,

Which dubs you the Chief of the Clan.
  May countrymen find,
  Its lightning behind,
A home in a far stranger lan'.

[*Gives the sword.*]

VICE PRESIDENTS.

  Vice Presidents, yours
  Are the President's powers
And duties when absent he's found.
  If with honors enrolled,
  High stations you hold,
See that for true worth you're renowned.

MANAGERS.

  Ye Managers five,
  Working-bees of the hive,
You transact all our business affairs;
  With shrewd common sense
  Our bounties dispense
In the way Constitution prepares.
  The stranger forfairn,
  The fatherless bairn,
The widow o'erburthened wi' cares,
  The emigrant novice,
  All—all 't is your office
To counsel, befriend, dry the tears.
  But the idle, the lazy,

The skellum, drunk-crazy,
(A shame to their Scottish forbears,)
Let them go to the guns—
They are bastards, not sons,
Undeserving our alms, or our prayers.

CHAPLAIN.

Our Chaplain comes next,
He will show what the text
Meaneth, "Mercy and not sacrifice,"
By soothing grief's sighing,
By cheering the dying,
And pointing to homes in the skies.
'T is also his place
At our feast to say grace,
And attend at our last obsequies.

PHYSICIAN.

Our honored Physician
Will find that his station
Will be to prescribe for the sick;
And if there is need,
Both to blister and bleed,
Or apply to the soles a warm brick;
Give his visits unbought,
And his pills all for naught;
Then hang them! wha says he 's a quack.

TREASURER.

To keep, sir, the funds
  Shall be yours, giving bonds
Approved of by Presidents all.
  Each dollar received,
  Expended, or saved
Book down, and report it withal.
  And in holding it fast,
  Take a hint frae the past—
Remember the break in Canal.

RECORDING SECRETARY.

You Scribe, the Recording,
  Good surety affording,
Give bonds, like the Treasurer, too,
  For you have in keeping,
  Of joy and of weeping
Our badges and bonnets o' blue.
  A list of the clan
  You shall keep to a man,
Collecting each fee and each due ;
  Give notice of meetings
  By messenger greetings
If needs be—tho' seldom, I trow.
  You 'll gie, sir, in short,
  An Annual· Report
Of doings all, flamingly true.

CORRESPONDING SECRETARY.

Our Scribe Corresponding,
In duties abounding,
Shall manage all foreign affairs ;
And when absent 's his billy
Will try to keep tally—
Assist him and lessen his cares.

TO ALL THE OFFICERS.

Now to your election
None making objection,
Be each in his office installed ;
Enter on the discharge ·
Of your duties at large,
Like those wha are worthily called.
In acting be careful—
In everything prayerful—
Oh, see that you 're never black-balled !

TO ALL THE SOCIETY.

To each St. Andrew's son
Ae word mair and I 've done :
These men are your choice—are they not ?
Then show them respect,
Assist them to act,
And brotherly kindness promote.

When into our book
Inspectors shall look,
May our names there be found without blot.
" Dues standing unpaid "
Let it never be said,
And for Charity's sake never wrote.
Then a relish, the best,
Shall be given our feast,
And with true honors dressed
Shall each one, in the sphere of his lot,
Be found a kind hearted, leal, brave, honest Scot.

ST. ANDREW'S FESTIVAL.

———

AN IMPROMPTU POEM READ AT THE ANNUAL GATHERING IN 1858.

———

" To kind Winslow's welcome cheer"—
Was the slogan of this year,
Calling clansmen far and near
     To their annual festival.
Hence, soon as the night set in,
Brawly decked in tartan sheen,
Lads and lasses might be seen
     Promenading in the hall.

When met th' Association
For officer 'stallation,
Was it not a grand occasion
     And quite worthy this my sang ?
In circle as ye ken them,
For Presidents this annum
Stood Kirky, Grannis, Denham,
     Three chieftains brave and strang.

Whitelaw, Downie, Mac, and Shanks,
With the chiel wha clinks their pranks,
Highest in the official ranks
    As Managers found place ;
While the Reverend James McGill
Did the Chaplain's station fill ;
And P. Gordon for his skill
    The Physician's niche did grace.

Nor shall it be forgot here
The Treasurer to note here,
For Davie is a Scot here,
    Honest as he's days auld.
Nor shall Watty too be missed, sir,
And Aleck—scribes the best, sir,
Tho' last upon the list, sir,
    Of those to be installed.

Here Inger, wi' decorum,
All their duties set before 'em
And wi' royal variorum
    He dubbed them all quite attic—
By the flourish of his sword,
By the fiat of his word,
Now they strut each one a lord,
    Tho' our gathering 's democratic.

After this, (we love to rhyme o't,)
They had a happy time o't,
Shaking hands and bearing min' o't—
     Dear hame and auld lang syne !
When in fancy wafted thither
To their native hills of heather,
Come a joy and grief together
     Scotchmen feel but can't define.

Everything was purely Scottish—
But " to supper " came the notice—
Sae the table round I wot is
     Besieged in a trice.
Hark !—we bargained for a knockit—
A bit piece like for our pocket—
But as much as we could look at
     Was ours, of dainties nice.

Hark ! the Chairman cries, " Peace, peace, now !
Let each screw up his face now
Till the Chaplain says the grace now
     At this our yearly feast !"
What an endless string o' dishes—
Cakes, and pies, and fruits, and fishes—
Served up a' to each ane's wishes—
     And the haggis—Winslow's best !

How grand to eat ane's supper,
While the pipes o' Tommy Coup-er
Sweetly play up " Tommy Tucker "
  All the senses steept in bliss !
Cleopatra in her barque, sir,
When visiting her Marc, sir,
For a' the poet's wark, sir,
   Was naught ava to this.

Whist ! whist ! thro' all our ranks, sir,
Is urged the silence branks, sir,
Till frien' Eaton rendered thanks, sir,
  For—the tentie waiters' capers.
And now see ! the Chairman startin'
To his feet in royal tartan
Gies the opening speech—a smart ane—
  Which see in to-morrow's papers.

Now, Kirkpatrickally given,
Was the chief toast of the even—
With its honors ten times seven
  Be it ours to cheer the luck !
Now in good loyal feeling,
And loud, loud as thunder pealing,
Was rent the very ceiling,
  With the healths of Vic and Buck.

Frien' Palmer rose and gave, sir,
A speech for Scots, the brave, sir,
Her poets and the lave, sir,
       Of literary name.
Nor was by him forgot, sir,
Americans of note, sir,
Who stand without a blot, sir,
       Upon the list o' fame.

Next Spalding, versed in story,
Was to speak o' Freedom's glory
And of battle-fields all gory
       With her victim patriots' fame.
Peace! peace, unto their manes!
To us—their sons—the gain is,
And ever to maintain this
       Should be our highest aim.

Next worthy Ingersoll, sir,
Spoke of Press, and Church, and School, sir,
Till one fancied ne'er a fool, sir,
       Could be here or yet at hame.
While guid Benedict, right witty,
Did extol the lasses pretty,
Yet gied skeletons their ditty
       For lacking tongue and wame.

Ye hae heard in hawthorn bush, sir,
The blackbird and the thrush, sir,
And the laverock's matin gush, sir,
  Up in the welkin's crest.
Well—here you 've also heard, sir,
A Falkoner and Bird, sir,
That has every passion stirred, sir,
  Within your stubborn breast.

Next Kerruish on his shanks, sir,
'Presents the thrifty Manx, sir,
With their hundreds in the banks, sir,
  Weel off are they these times.
Frien' Schuttlem, for the Dutchmen,
Did feel at hame wi' Scotchmen,
And fervent prays that such men,
  May aye hae routh o' dimes.

Loudly called on was the Mayor,
But his Honor was not there—
The bard said his head was sair—
  Sae he had to gang to bed.
Alack ! for such a rumor—
We hae lost his wit and humor—
But frien' Prosser wi' his hammer,
  Did gie a stroke instead.

A health to our gen'rous host, sir,
Sparing neither pains nor cost, sir,
He has made our feast a boast, sir,
  And worth remembrance aye.
Now finally we adjourn, sir,
For to tak' a dancing turn, sir,
Then part at peep o' morn, sir,
  To meet next Andrew's Day.

THE LEGEND OF ST. ANDREW.

READ AT THE ST. ANDREW'S FESTIVAL, 1859.

Say, Scottish Muse, for legend famed,
How came St. Andrew to be named
   Auld Scotland's tutelar Saint?
While thus her lads and lasses meet
His festival to celebrate
   Wi' native glee and chant,
To hear the mythic tale related—
If time and patience will permit it—
   Is just the thing we want.

'Twas in the days of cruel Nero,
Wha butchered mony a Christian hero,
When Rome, then " mistress of the world,"
Tried hard to hae her flag unfurl'd
O'er Scotia's hills, whom Fate, to ennoble,
Had stampt for ay the unconquerable,
There lived a man in ancient Fife,
Ane ERIC called, a worthy chief.

Oft had he marched to battle-field,
And Roman legion back repelled.
ALBION, the young and brave, his son,
Six times the palm had also won;
And times as often sat enthroned
Under the "SACRED OAK" renowned—
The grateful pæan's lofty swell
Re-echoing thro' the rocky dell.

But as the foe to war was drilled,
And better armed to take the field,
Our chieftain and his faithfu' band
Were whiles put to a desperate stand.
'Twas after ane o' those hard scenes
That ERIC and his tribe convenes;
An armistice must be obtained
Or Scotland's freedom's at an end.
Reduced to ruin's very brink,
Each wot not what to say or think;
A silent anguish rent the breast,
When ERIC, rising, thus his friends addressed:

"Alternative none,
But slavery's groan!
Sons of the wildwood! what must be done?
To end this sad strife
Wha offers his life
A sacrifice to the usurper's knife?

Has the land of our birth
Nae child to step forth,
And willingly bleed for our homes and our hearth?
The gods are displeased,
And they must be appeased,
Or Scotland by ruthless impiety's seized.
For our sires' gray hairs—
For our children's young years—
For our mothers', and sisters', and wives' holy tears—
For our country's glory—
On her altar all gory
Wha dies the meek victim, immortal in story?"

He paused for some one.   But not long.
Young ALBION rose amid the throng
And cheerful answer thus returned,
While all the patriot in him burned:

"This honor be mine;
My life I consign
To foeman, the Roman, and Odin divine.
Fellow-soldiers, adieu!
Let 'AIRY HALL' view—
Ever mark you for your country the brave and the true;
May it never be known
That her cause was undone
For the lack of a sacrifice free, to atone."

He goes—nor waits a mother's kissing—
A country's thanks—a Druid's blessing.
The Roman camp, ta'en in surprise,
Receives the willing sacrifice.
Such self-devotedness and zeal
For liberty, for country's weal,
Was not without regard beheld
By foe who oft had met his shield.
To wait his fate some after day
The cohort bears him proud away
To the drear donjon of a tower
Which overlooked the neighboring shore.
  'Twas on November, night the last,
That ALBION into jail was cast;
Lorn, dank, and dismal was his cell—
Fit place for sad despair to dwell;
Gyves, tools of torture and of death,
Hung all around—infernal graith!
The chiseled rock, on farther side,
Table, and chair, and bed supplied;
While thro' the grated winnock shone,
Bright on the floor, the silver moon.
Of fellow-prisoners, nane were there
To shorten time and banish care
With sympathetic converse, save
An aged man, cheerful, yet grave.
Awhile both o' them pensive sat;
At last the elder thus commenced the chat:

"Peace! son of the mountain, the wildwood, and glen;
May I not inquire what's the cause of thy chain?
Your bearing, so noble, bespeaks you a youth
Not suffering for crime, but for right and the truth."

ALBION—

"If, honored stranger, the lifting of spear
For freedom be wrong, then for crime I am here.
For country beloved! I hail these abodes,
A propitiation to Rome and the gods."

ELDER—

"To die for one's countrymen, truly is brave,
But far more so to suffer, one's en'my to save;
And such a great hero I've come to proclaim
To you and your countrymen, JESU by name."

ALBION—

"You're then that St. Andrew who brought, with the foe,
Strange gods into Scotland, a short time ago.
The hours pass on slowly—the morrow, who knows—?
Come, tell us your 'story, and preach us the Cross."

ST. ANDREW—

"Most gladly, my son, for to this same intent,
From the city Jerusalem divinely I'm sent;
My mission here done, at Petræa I'm found*
To seal with my death the great truths I propound."

---

* "At Petræa I'm found." It was at this place, a city of Achaia, that our
Apostle suffered martyrdom, at the hand of Ægeas, the Roman proconsul.
To make his death more lingering, he was crucified on a cross like the letter
X—tied to it instead of nailing.

But it would be too profuse
In the legendary Muse,
Andrew's sermon all to tell,
Or on his experience dwell.
Let suffice it :—Ere he ended,
By the grace o' Gude befriended,
ALBION in the Christian's creed
Was a convert true, indeed !
In an ecstasy of soul
Renovated now in whole ;
Not the savage warrior song
But the saint's employs his tongue.

" O wonderful story ! unparalleled love !
The Lord of glory descends from above ;
Takes on him man's nature, to suffer and die,
That a lost sinful creature might praise him on high !
But say, did he suffer a sacrifice free,
And send such an offer of mercy to me ?
O ! welcome the donjon, the Cross' shame and pain—
All—aught, if I, undone, the crown but attain !
In works all deficient !   How weak my belief !
But Christ's all-sufficient, and so I am safe.
For baptism, washing the soul of its sin,
Yon water is gushing—may I not be clean ?"

At the east end of their cell,
From the rock-clift, water fell,

In the moonbeam sparkling bright;
Thither both repair'd, and straight
Was performed 'the sacred rite.
Silence eloquent did reign,
Till the Apostle thus again :

" Pointed out by the Baptist at Jordan's famed ford,
Well do I remember first finding my Lord,
And from that day to this it has been my chief aim
To preach him to others and bring them to Him;
With miracles many, with wonder and sign,
Confirming my mission and gospel divine.
But now the day breaketh, and night flies away :
Lest preaching the gospel impede Cæsar's sway
I've here been confined, and to-day I must sail
On the ' Castor and Pollux," or death is my bail.
Heaven's ways are mysterious—good out of evil
Is oftimes the issue, and foiled is the devil.
Adieu ! my young brother, sweet fruit of my toil !
First convert to JESU in this your far isle !
Should earthly fame leave you, and dear friends disown,
Hold fast your profession, eye fixed on the crown.
We part—and no more in this body we meet ;
Yet our spirits hereafter each other will greet,
And our bones* rest together where now stand our feet.

---

* In A. D. 370, it is said that a monk of Petræa, in Achaia, warned by a
vision, sailed westward until he landed at St. Andrew's, in Scotland. Here
he founded a chapel and tower, near the spot where our two heroes were

Commissioned of Heaven, o'er Scotland's domain,
As tutelar angels, forever we 'll reign ;
To watch o'er her liberty civil, is thine—
To foster and guard her religious, is mine.
' The hated religion,' our hopeless like cause,
Two centuries hence has the shield of the laws ;
The instrument used for our torture and death,
The ensign of Scotland and badge of her faith.
My last day and best day—the last of November—
Prince, peasant, and pauper will ever remember.
Rapt into the future, O Scotland ! I see
The Cross o'er thy hills waving glorious and free !
Druidic false worship all vanished away,
Like the mist of the dawn at the rising of day !
As race follows race down the vista of time
Thy sons in the arts stand the chief in each clime !
A blessing to mankind, thy martyr divine,
Thy patriot hero, and sweet poet shine !"

The warden now for the preacher stands,
And they ship him away to some ither lands ;

---

imprisoned. The tower is still standing, and is one of the most ancient edi-
fices in Scotland. There is a cave in front of it which bears the name of St.
Andrew, ten feet square, and hewed out of the rock. On one side is a stone
altar, and an inner den which perhaps served as a sleeping apartment for the
monk. His name is said to be St. Rule or St. Regulus. He first colonized
the metropolitan see of Scotland, etc. It is also affirmed by tradition that he
brought the relics of St. Andrew, after they had been twice disinterred, and
buried them finally in his cave. We only add, that about the same time,
when Christianity became popular, the bones of Albion were found and
deposited in the same place.

ALBION before the General goes,
To wait the word that his days would close;
But his tale so simple, and yet so brave,
Inclined the heart of a Roman to save.

"Attention!" he called, and his look was stern;
"I want you to go to your ancient cairn
And tell your father to save his bairn
By signing this parchment, that Cæsar 's king,
And our troops we 'll withdraw, nor tax you a thing.
A people so brave takes a Roman to prize—
We want but to have you honored allies."

The youth, quite thoughtful, shook his head,
And, hesitatingly, thus said:

"Yes—if my country first had been
        The fell aggressor,
I, prevalent, might return again
        An intercessor.
But—'tis no use.   O, Romans, know!
        The independent
My father lives, or by the foe
        Dies, the defendant!
You urge me: well, I go to die,
        And serve my nation;
To tell them all about the joy
        Of my salvation."

It was not long, on the wings of love,
Till he joined his friends in "the sacred grove."
He told them his message, they ey'd him askance;
He spoke of the Cross, and they bristled the lance!
Estranged were the hearts of his nearest kin
As he prayed his God to forgive their sin.
On his honored teacher's decussate beam,
In the sight of the foe they crucify him.

Thus died this patriot Christian youth,
Scotland's first convert and martyr for truth.
His blood stained the heather, hence purple its bloom;
Hence mighty the heroes that snuff its perfume;
Hence many and noble the martyr-dead
That glorious rest 'neath its gentle shade.

SCOTCH PICTURES.

READ AT THE ST. ANDREW'S FESTIVAL, 1860.

Dear honored friends and countrymen!
November's last returns again
  And seats us at our feast—
Which serves in place the happy scene
Of weddin, kirn, or Hallowe'en
  In early days possest.
Thrown to the winds be then all care,
  And for an hour at least
Let's Scottish stamp the present cheer
  And hail each worthy guest,
   Believing we 're living
    Yet callants in the glen;
   Or sporting, and courting
    The lasses—as ye ken.

Land o' our calf-gang! when we still
Think of thee, how our thrapples fill,
  And find a vent in sighin';

So captive Jews beside the burns
Of Babel grat and sang in turns,
    Remembering their Zion.
Yes, Caledonia, tho' thou art
    A step-dame rather cruel,
Yet in thy every bairnie's heart
        Thou 'rt still for a' the jewel.
            Thy mountains, thy fountains,
                Thy heather, birk, and broom,
            Still warm us and charm us
                Where'er on earth we roam.

Come, let us climb yon rugged steep,
And at the landscape take a peep—
    Wide stretching to the sea;
Lo! shining lakes and rivers flow;
Plantations variegated grow;
    Corn fields and pasture-lea.
'Mid aspens rise the haunted tower
    Where restless ghosts are seen;
In yonder dell, at midnight hour,
    Fairies to dance convene.
            Renowned there that ground there
                For Freedom's claymore strong!
            No place seen but has been
                The patriot minstrel's song.

D' ye see yon cottage up the moors?
The reek to heaven mute-curling towers

Like incense o' the morn.
Before the door on gowany green
The mither wi' the bairns are seen,
      Claes hanging on the thorn;
Behind 's the peat-stack divot-thatched,
      And bortree fenced kail-yard;
Crummie to loup the dyke is watched
      By Snap that sits the hird.
            On bobbin' twig, Robbin
               Does o'er his gamut run,
            While under, see! yonder
               The cat thrums in the sun.

      *   *   *   *   *

Schule 's out—and its the afternoon
Of Saturday, the month o' June,
      And scholars jauk and play;
Some up the lin are guddlin' trout,
Some thro' the glade are in pursuit
      Of nests and posies gay.
When do we first begin to love?
      Wee Tammy crowns his Jean
With rushy cap in meadow grove,
      Nae happier king or queen!
            Baith modest, the oddest
               Thoughts cross the spotless mind,
            Revealing young feeling
               That's hard to be defined.

Will sits astride the fauld-sod-dyke;
Bees round him dart wi' desperate fyke—
　　But he must taste their sweet.
Jock fights a wasp-bink like a Turk,
Till stabb'd wi' mony a poisoned dirk
　　He makes a base retreat.
A score at cricket on the croft
　　Skip thro' among the whins;
Anither squad wi' jackets dofft,
　　At shinny peel their shins.
　　　　With jumping and romping
　　　　　　Unbounded are their plays;
　　　　How glorious, victorious,
　　　　　　Are schoolboy Saturdays!

"Let's mak' our hay while shines the sun"—
Down the smooth meadow there is fun;
　　Say taste they not the bottle?
Five brawny chiels keep "chap-and-strake"—
The spratty swathes lie in their wake,
　　But breathing now they whittle.
And farther down a motley band
　　Of cotter, hind, and maiden,
Keep jeering ane another bland,
　　While raking, coleing, teadin.
　　　　Ha! Sanny fair Nanny
　　　　　　Pursues, till trip—she falls
　　　　To have him—behave him—
　　　　　　For hark! the master calls.

O'er moorlan', fell, and braes of heather
The shepherd ca's his ewes together :
    Day o'er the mountains breaking.
See ! how his colly doth fulfill
The sign or whistle of his will,
    Not even once mistaking.
Urged jostling to the washing pond
    Ane o'er the brink they push in,
Anon, ten thousand after bound
    And get a fearfu' swashin'.
      Niest borne there, they 're shorn there
        For rent o' a' their claes ;
      While speaned there, unstained there,
        Lambs baaing climb the braes.

At the invasion of their peace
The tenants of the wilderness
    Show symptoms of alarm ;
The muir-fowl flutter o'er their brood ;
The hares scud to the scroggie wood,
    Scared from their cozy form ;
The peesweeps loud their choler vent,
    Wings flapping in a bustle ;
While the lang-nebbed whaup's complaint
    Is heard in dolefu' whistle.
      All 's drearie—nought's cheerie,
        Except the laverock gay,
      That fearless and peerless
        Mid-heaven pours forth his lay !

ODE TO THE REPUBLIC.

———

READ AT THE ST. ANDREW'S FESTIVAL, 1861, IN RESPONSE TO
TOAST, "U. S. AMERICA."

———

Hail ! land of cataract,
Prairie, wood, river, lake,
       Vast and sublime !
Who would not sing of thee,
Destined the home to be
Of all the nations, free, ·
       Down through all time ?

From the Atlantic tide
To the Pacific, wide
       Stretches thy sway ;
Mountains of snowy top,
Valleys of sunny slope
Waving with every crop
       Crown thee for aye !

Young, yet for high deserts
Sage in the liberal arts!
        See, hand in hand,
Justice with upright scale,
Industry, public zeal,
Love, peace, and temperance hale,
        March through the land!

Favored by nature, thine
Is the enriching mine,
        Soil, lake, and river;
Hence comfort cheers thy hearth;
Hence over all the earth
Thy independent worth
        Is honored ever!

Guide of the pilgrim flock
Safe to old Plymouth Rock,
        Long tempest driven,
Still be their children's guide;
Through every turbid tide
May the republic ride,
        Anchored in heaven!

A SCOTCHMAN'S PORTRAIT.

READ BEFORE THE ST. ANDREW'S SOCIETY, 1862.

Leaving to curious speculation
To say, if character formation
Be molded by organization
    Or circumstance,
The traits o' Scotchmen and their nation
    We just advance.

Sprung frae the gods, true legends said,
Were beth their mither and their dad,
Yet some hae since the Roman raid*
    Got up a clatter,
To prove them but of Celtic breed
    Come o'er the water.

---

* The invasion of Julius Cæsar.

But be this as it may, a race
They were renowned for sense and grace,
That sinks the present frozen face
          Down under zero;
Wha can withhold the meed o' praise
          Frae Ossian's hero?

In form, like to his mountain clift—
Gigantic tow'ring in the lift;
In genius, like his eagle swift—
          Of piercing ken;
In battle, like the whirling drift
          Adown his glen.

The open forehead, stern yet fair;
The nose and cheekbone high and spare;
The dark blue eye; the gouden hair,
          And whiskers red,
Bespoke his was the soul to dare
          Decisive deed!

Nor is our chieftain of the clan,
A modern sample bad of man;
When in his native garb he's drawn,
          Wi' broad claymore,
Plumed bonnet, kilt, and tartan gran',
          He'll daunt a score!

Time out o' date, 't has been confessed,
A Highland welcome is the best;
To stranger as to friend, the feast
   Is kindly spread :
Even the fell foe is made his guest
   When found in need.

Save his blaeberries on the bent,
Hame luxuries are rather scant ;
Still wi' his wiffie quite content,
   And sweet wee Meggies,
He breaks his bannock, and can vaunt
   O'er guid fat haggis !

His sports are manly, as the chase,
But Curliania fun's the spice
That makes his winters taste sae nice ;
   While up ilk strath
The kirk, wi' Calvinistic grace,
   Tolls his true faith.

To him nae music's void o' charms,
But chief, his soul the pibroch warms ;
He canna sit its war alarms
   And not advance,
Nor list his fiddle's tickling thairms
   Without the dance.

Phrenologists say that his skull
Has twa-three bumps that's mair than full—
Hence 't is nae wonder spaewives gull
  And sights unthrive him,
Or that he's sic a stubborn mull
  As nane can drive him.

Up in the warl' he gets a lift,
Sometimes by mother wit and thrift;
For rhyming, too, he's got the gift,
  And art o' thinking;
Yet his best friends hae ca'd him daft
  For whisky drinking.

A lover o' his native hearth
He's found on every clime on earth,
Often esteemed for sterling worth
  And honest fame;
Yet whiles, by lacking pride o' birth,
  His country's shame.

Thus much for Scotland's lads and asses.
Ae stave just for her bonnie lasses;
Of a' the fair, our Burns them classes
  Creation's boast!
Sae, jolly bachelors, fill your glasses
  And drink the toast!

'T wad ill become sons o' the heather,
Frae hame thus met wi' ane anither,
Not to remember their auld mither
      And sweethearts dear !
Here's, then, the sex ! wi'—a' the gether—
      Three hearty cheers !

SCOTCH AITS.

———

READ AT THE ST. ANDREW'S FESTIVAL, 1863, IN RESPONSE TO THE TOAST, "SCOTLAND—THE LAND O' CAKES."

———

Of Scotland's corn, her aits we sing
While met together banqueting
On Cleveland's every dainty thing
     And nature's best;
Borne hame on memory's fitful wing
     Let's swell the feast.

When vernal shower revives the sod
Gran' peeps the braird aboon the clod;
Gran' when in ragging it doth nod
     First the tap-pickle;
But grander far, when ripe, its load
    .Falls 'neath the sickle!

How changed in native look and size
Is Scotland's corn 'neath Yankee skies.
Shrunk in the shot-blade, here it dies
        A still-born cereal;
A peck o' which wad not suffice
        To bake ae *farl!*

While some esteem the staff of life
To be the beer or wheaten sheaf,
And ithers hold it their belief
        That rice or maize is,
The true-bred Scotchman, as the chief,
        Gives *aits* his praises.

And well he may, for 't is the corn
He sips at soon as he is born;
His mither 'neath his chin doth turn
        The soft white towel,
And dits his gab—despite his spurn—
        Wi' *water-gruel.*

And when at schule, a laddie learning,
Sometimes, right hurried in the morning,
He has been kenned, the hour returning,
        To tine his carritch,
Yet never to need double warning
        To tak' his *parritch.*

To seal the fates o' Hallowe'en
What was the jovial supper ta'en?
And what the ten-hour on the green
   Besprent wi' gowans,
At peat-moss, or at harvest scene?
   What but the *sowans?*

At public dinner wi' oration;
At kirn or wedding celebration;
At every social, great occasion,
   The table's luggies.
Was wanting in the numeration
   Without the *haggis.*

When, for the dawrk, to mak' ane strang,
Or when frae hame ane had to gang,
To make the journey no seem lang,
   A noble tonic
Was in the pouch, of cheese a whang
   And guid steeve *bannock!*

To hungry weans that aye wad eat;
To meet the call o' friends and treat;
To the invalid, that dainty meat
   And cordial shuns,
What's half sae guid, or tastes sae sweet
   As souple *scones?*

Mere teethless mummies, dwarf'd in size,
Let epicurean bodies prize
Their sugar'd cookies, buns, and pies,
    But for the sake
Of country, let a Scotchman's choice
    Be *crampy cake!*

What makes a Scotchman nothing dread?
In weal or woe haud up his head?
What makes his step the giant's tread,
    Daunting his foes?
What but his being hardy fed
    On fat *kail brose?*

When Beefie fell beneath the axe,
And Grumphy squealed to pay the tax,
Rare ornaments adorned the bauks
    As mart and hadden;
Nae better kitchen did ane ask
    Than the *white puddin!*

When summer wet, bro't harvest bad,
The barley crap a failure sad!
A welcome substitute and glad
    Was the shell'd oats;
To boil the pot, the guidwife had
    Her nievfu' *groats.*

Sown anywhere—on sunny slope,
Or on the mountain's heathery top,
Aits never blight the farmer's hope
    In fother-feed;
While cottar hail them as his crop
    For *haver bread.*

To guard, on harvest-morn, the head
Of hundred tassels, all arrayed
With sparkling dew-drop—frae the reid
    Of sparrow rowdy,
The hird-boy pipes his oaten-reed
    Yaup for his *crowdie.*

Let Scotchmen now a bumper fill
Fresh frae the burn, and lest it chill
Shake on it just a little meal,
    Then toom the horn
" To Scotland's everlasting weal,
    And *aits* her corn!"

ANNUAL REPORT OF THE ST. ANDREW'S SOCIETY 1864.

If asked was the question, of money received,
Wha hae the last towmond by such been relieved?
This wad be the answer, nine cases in ten,
It has been the puir soldier, his wife, or his wean.

On Janar' the first, 'midst the sleet and the storm,
A lassie, frae Canada, begged to get warm;
For some ane o' Cleveland her husband was gane
A substitute South and left her alane;
Aside, it was whispered, " to tame her a shrew."
She spak the Scotch tongue and her story seem'd true,
We could na but gie her a dollar or two.
Sae we helped a wee, being right weel aware
A Scotch beggar, worthy, in Cleveland was rare.

The next wha did pray for relief frae our Saint
Was Bridget, wi' childer all three, and in want;
Her story was told in a rich Irish brogue,
While she swore by St. Patrick she came not *in cog*.

Her man, ca'd McDonnal, a Highlander born,
To our bounty endowed her and childer forlorn.
To carry the hud, or to work on the farm,
Ill-suited the soul of a patriot warm !
In the " garb of old Gaul " he strode forth in his glory
And, landing at Shiloh, fell—ending his story !
Her tale so heroic, we could na' forbear
To gie her five dollars and lighten her care,

Next twa both together, wi' dudded bairns six,
Made urgent appeal—in a desperate fix !
In search of employment frae York State they came,
Their men in the army and starved out at hame.
Back—objects of censure, as well as of pity—
We sent them again by the help of our city.
And here we would heartily tender our thanks
To those who assist us though not of our ranks.
If Charity ever embodied has been,
It is in the person of Jonathan's Queen !

    Next, early in Summer G——t made us a ca'.
Of naval engagements, O how he did blaw !
He'd got on the Essex, while fighting wi' Foote—
The dauntless, Gude-fearing—a sair scaulded snout.
He also wi' Farragut—bravest of tars !—
Had gotten some four or five glorious scars !
Besides in his youth he had played 'mang the heather,
Sae we treat him, of course, ·a true chieftain and brither.

There came one in harvest, his name Willie B——,
He had been through all the Potomac campaign.
Its runs, gaps, burghs, ridges, each furnished a theme
For story to blazon the deeds of his fame!
On the Mountain Lookout, 'bove the clouds and the storms,
'Midst the carnage of battle and roar of alarms,
He was ane of the heroes that flung to the breeze
The star-striped banner, which streamed—if you please,
Norther lights to illumine with Freedom and Truth
The rebel, benighted, slave States of the South.
And then in his youth he had strolled 'mang the broom,
Sae we treat him, of course, as a son returned home.

About the same time, on a Saturday night,
Wanting board over Sabbath, appeared a sad wight,
Misfortune's own child!—at the bloody Ringgold.
Both an arm and a foot he had lost, we were told;
Too crippled to work, his last shift was too beg,
Wi' dangling coat-sleeve and a stiff wooden leg.
And then in his youth he had gathered the slaes,
And pu'd the blaeberries on breckony braes:
Sae we treat him, of course, while he in a clean sark
To show he was grateful, gied wi' us to kirk.

One case mair must suffice, lest we weary your patience,
'T was one wha in Libby had lived without rations;
A band of guerrillas, from out o' the thicket,
At midnight surprised him, on duty, a picket.

How better by far had he died midst the strife
Than have borne, from the merciless, prisoner life!
Dank dungeons, diseases, filth, famine nigh death,
Had so changed a brither—he looked like a wraith.
On crutches, all weak, it was too much a task
To answer in whispers what pity might ask.
He sighed for Vermont—for the loved ane at home.
Alas! in our Woodland he rests in his tomb.
Of the battle he bore not so much as one scar,
Yet we wept as we thought on the horrors of war;
Of wives and of mithers bereft of their hope;
Of sisters and children deprived of their prop.
Oh! when shall our fightings and feuds have an end,
   Oppression and discord be heard of no more,
And peace again o'er us her olive extend,
   Right reigning respected from shore unto shore?

A GRATEFUL WELCOME HOME TO OUR SOLDIERS.

READ AT THE ST. ANDREW'S FESTIVAL, 1865.

Union soldiers of the North!
  Welcome to our feast you come,
Crowned with victory, peace, and worth.
  Glorious heroes, welcome home!
We would, of your presence proud,
Hearty speak our gratitude.

Promptly at your country's call
  Buckled was the harness on;
Home and its endearments all
  Sacrificed without a moan;
Bounty sought not, nor bestowed,
Bankrupts public gratitude.

Thro' our fell vexatious wars,
   Hardship, danger, death were braved
That the Federal Stripes and Stars
   Aye might grace the Union saved.
Sure such matchless fortitude
Claims eternal gratitude.

So you 've crushed the rebel South ;
   Laughed to scorn its chivalry.
Armed in justice, might, and truth,
   Clean wiped out its slavery.
Yes ! and hosts of freedmen loud
Joyful shout their gratitude.

Now that you have peace restored,
   In some public office rest,
Always at the festive board
   Honored as a worthy guest,
Fighting o'er again each feud,
'Mid the applause of gratitude.

By our blood and treasure spilt ;
   By our prisoners' martyrdom ;
Never shall secession's guilt
   Curse again our land—our home ;
Ever vigilant and shrewd,
We shall show our gratitude.

8

If the graves of our loved ones,
   Hallowed have the tyrant's sod,
Never more shall Slavery's groans
   Pierce the ear of Freedom's God.
To all time, our land renewed
Sings of love and gratitude.

Some, alas! come sick and maimed—
   Would we had the power to heal!
Well, the greater are you famed,
   And the more for you we feel.
Wounds and scars for country's good,
Pity claims, and gratitude.

Bravest patriots! cheer up!
   If you have our battles fought—
Been in darkest hours our hope,
   Shall we let you lack for aught?
You and yours have shares endowed
In our all with gratitude.

And the fallen!—not the dead—
   Blazoned on a nation's page,
All due honors to them paid,
   They survive from age to age,
With their spirit more imbued
And increasing gratitude.

Merchants may with craftsmen toil;
  Statesmen scheme, and churchmen pray;
Farmers sow and reap the soil;
  But a country's pith and stay
Is the soldier, whose heart's blood
Streams for it in gratitude.

TO THE CLANS OF CUYAHOGA.

———

READ BEFORE THE ST. ANDREW'S SOCIETY.

——

Beneath the Union Stripes and Stars,
  The Clan Cuyahoga holds a gatherin';
Not for redress of wrangs or wars,
  But for "the chat o' peace" as brethren ;
And patriotic call to min'
The happy days o' auld-lang-syne.

When Adam first was made, 't was seen
  That he himself alane was no man,
Sae to perfect the thing, I ween,
  A help-meet formed was lovely woman.
Hence, traits beth social and domestic
Crown human nature all majestic !

But how it comes the Scottish race
   Is mair gregarious than ithers
We dinna' ken—yet Yankee guess,
   'Tis thro' the clanship o' their fathers,
Whose love o' hame and social fun
Is still the heirship o' their son.

Nae true born Scotchman can forget
   The hallowed scenes o' Caledonia,
Tho' it should be his after fate
   To soop the lums o' Pandemonia,
Or roll in luxury—hae at leisure
In fields Elysian a' his pleasure.

What tho' he pu's beneath these skies
   The peach, the grape, and melon juicy,
Mair sweet by far does he not prize
   His native slae and berries racy,
Which he in youth was wont to gather,
Up briery glen and hill o' heather.

Beloved land! place o' our birth
   And childhood's dear associations!
Contrasted with those joys and worth
   Say, what are a' these Yankee notions?
One evening round our father's hearth
Is worth a lifetime o' sic mirth!

Should poortith or distress assail
　　Some honest countryman and brither,
Let beacons blaze on ilka hill,
　　And to the rescue, clansmen gather;
The pibroch, or the coronach,
Attendant ever on life's tract.

Dear brither countrymen! in youth,
　　Ere dreaming we would cross the water,
Did we not learn the cheering truth
　　Of a far country called the better!
Weel! may we ane and a' there meet
In social circle, still mair sweet!

THE SPRIG OF HEATHER.

———

Lines written on receiving a Sprig of Heather enclosed in
a Letter from the Rev. Dr. W. H. Goodrich, on his tour
through Scotland, and read before the St. Andrew's
Society, 1869.

———

Eh !—come frae Scotland, our auld mither,
Pu'd in its bloom, a sprig of heather,
A rare memento, frae nane ither
          Than our kind Pastor,
That to recruit his health 's gane thither,
          And serve his Master.

Tho' but a trifle in itsel',
Yet how much for him it doth tell—
While like a wand of magic spell
          It brings before us
Home-scenes of mountain, muir, and dell,
          Wi' a' their stories.

While botanists at large descant
About the genus o' the plant,
'T is ours in homely rhyme to chaunt
   Its modest fame,
Coeval and concomitant
    Wi' Scotia's name.

A full half cent'ry 's come and fled
Since o'er the muirlan's was my tread
—My overcoat the checker'd plaid—
   Still ever green
In memory's waste is yet portrayed
    The varied scene.

Say, grew this twig upon the steep
Where Covenanters had to creep?
Or where the Brownies played bo-peep
   Under the moon,
Shearing the craps and faulding sheep
    For brose and shune?

A worthless shrub?—ah ! dinna sneer
Till ance about it mair ye hear;
Scotland wad not be Scotland dear
   Did not the heather
Wave round her brows sae princely fair
    —A pheasant feather.

What!—wot ye not that thro' the year
Such yields baith food and shelter rare
To outlier sheep, goat, deer, and hare;
    While to the grouse
And ither birds that fan the air
      'Tis crib and house?

Wha of us hae not to our father
Wi' thraw crook twined the rape o' heather,
Mair teuch and lasting than the teather
    Of hempen brand,
Wearing meanwhile the brog o' leather
    By heather tann'd.

The best o' butter 's frae the cow
That 's pastured on the heather knowe;
The best o' honey's frae the blow
    Of August heather;
And the best besom 's frae the cowe
    Of ling, its brither.

Yon cottage at his lordship's gate
Is heather-thatched, to be mair neat;
It's inmates feel (I 'm free to say 't)
    On couch of heather.
Mair comfort than the pampered great
    On beds of feather.

Its very smell is healing balm;
Of victory 'tis the glorious palm;
And its green sprout distill'd in alum
   Dyes gold the tartan—
Theme of the chieftain's loudest psalm,
   Courage impartin'.

Nae wonder that the clans of old
" Froach eilen "* made their slogan bold,
Or caused the heather flaunt in gold
   On badge and banner
The symbol recognized, which told
   Of health and honor.

Turn where one may, height, moss, and dell
Of Truth and Freedom stories tell:
Here, men the bravest did repel
   Usurpation's rod;
There, during persecution, fell
   The saints of God.

  * * * * * * *

The lark up-singing meets the dawn;
The hares sport amorous on the lawn;
Across the glade fleet bounds the fawn;
   And the peesweep
Doth, for her nest, the herd boy fan
   Wi' whisking sweep.

---

* " Heather Isle," the war cry.

The corbie croaks perch'd on the cairn;
The heron stalks among the fern;
Frae dizzy cliff the eagle stern
      Surveys his prey;
As dashing o'er the linn the burn
        Shines whitened spray.

Ohio, in thy sunny bowers
There 's mony bonnie flaunting flowers,
Which while we grateful prize as ours,
      We oft would rather
On native Caledonia's moors
        Snuff the pure heather.

Her very wilds in purple bloom
And shed afar a sweet perfume;
Beautiful land is that our home,
      Flora's own shrine;
Type of the heavenly yet to come;
        Say, yours and mine?

THE OLD AND NEW HOMES.

SUNG AT THE ST. ANDREW'S FESTIVAL, 1871. AIR—"SCOTTISH KAIL BROSE."

On the day of St. Andrew's, our Thanksgiving day,
Come let us as Scotch-Yankee brithers essay
For national mercies some fit grateful lay—
  O, the dear hames of auld Scotland,
  And O, for Ohio hames gay.

Our Scotch pilgrim fathers set wisely apart,
This day for expression of gladness of heart—
Memento of freedom, peace, joy, and desert—.
  O, the dear hames of auld Scotland,
  And O, for Ohio hames smart.

Like the Psalmist of old we can lilt at our feast
That the lines to us fallen are good, better, best—
That ours is the nation of nations confessed!
  O, the dear hames of auld Scotland,
  And O, for Ohio hames blest.

What land 's like the lands of the lochs and the lakes?
Like the lands of the johnnie and oaten crump cakes,
Or of schules, kirks, and Sabbath days that the man makes?
    O, the dear hames of auld Scotland,
    And O, for Ohio hames' sakes.

For the land that we left, and the land that we live in,
To which, shall we say, we owe everything, even,
Let praises ascend up forever to Heaven!
    O, the dear hames of auld Scotland,
    And O, for Ohio hames given.

Then here 's to braes o' the broom and heather,
And here 's to the lawns' of the Buckeye, together!
This ane our best friend, and that ither our mither.
    O, the dear hames of auld Scotland,
    And O, for Ohio hames brither!

TO THE MEMORY OF OUR DEPARTED BROTHERS.

ST. ANDREW'S FESTIVAL, 1871.

Ah·! our dear departed brothers,
  Solemn silence speaks our woe !
Now their place is filled by others !
  Who 's the next to follow ?—who ?

With us from our first formation,
  Present at each festival,
Nobly have they filled each station,
  Honored and beloved by all.

Patriotic, unassuming,
  Charitable to a fault,
All they said or did becoming—
  How their exit makes us halt !

Not alone are we bereaved;
　Family circles for them weep,
Hopeless? no, no; they believed,
　And in Jesus fell asleep.

Now no more our meetings cheering
　With their voice or deeds of love,
They are gone to more endearing
　Fellowship with saints above.

Yes, our dear departed brothers!
　Solemn silence speaks our woe;
But we join you soon with others,
　Parting never more to know.

A WORD OF ADVICE.

READ BEFORE THE ST. ANDREW'S SOCIETY, 1872.

My Yankee callants, ever dear,
  At this our social meeting
We would wi' moral lesson cheer,
And not wi' pulpit dogmas drear
  Be ane anither greeting.

'Tis granted that in memory still
  Youth's play-grounds loom before ye—
Auld Scotia's classic loch and rill,
Her granite cliff and heather hill,
  Bright wi' romantic story.

Kind mither's admonitions sage
  You hae not left behind you?
O practice down to hirplin' age,
Those truths which from the sacred page
  She oft wi' prayers enjoined you!

And this nae doubt was that you might
   The love of country fan—
Make ye the abler in life's fight
Stand up and battle for the right—
   Be everywhere the man !

Clear have we steered thro' childhood's gins;
   Ay, but there 's yet before us
In coming years, strange outs and ins—
Allurements and besetting sins,
   That may at last o'erpower us.

In every stage of life there is
   A something that's ascendant ;
To manage or mismanage this
(A target which to hit or miss)
   Makes weel or woe attendant.

In jostling thro' the busy crowd,
   Let not your course be aimless.
Beth for your ain and ithers' good
Some calling ought to be pursued
   That's honorable and blameless.

Govern your buying by your sales;
   On tide of speculation
Spread not at first too wide your sails,
Lest fooled by fogs and adverse gales
   You wreck your reputation.

9

And lest upon the quicksand banks
  Of bankruptcy you 're grounded,
Look well to commerce in her cranks;
And see your depths of trade and stanks
  Of debts be duly sounded.

To use deceit—to practise stealth,
  Imposing and extorting,
Is daubing character wi' filth—
Is hoarding curses up wi' wealth
  To damn acquired fortune.

To insure success in what you may,
  Of time disdain to borrow.
Whatever laziness may say
Leave not undone aught of to-day
  To mar that of to-morrow.

That you get rich we don't advise,
  Nor wish you great attendance;
Boys, this for you may not be wise;
But justly try to rise, and rise
  To manly independence.

As much of fame and peace depend
  On wha you mak' companions;
See such to virtue are inclined;
Obliging, faithful, honored, kind—
  Look out for sordid minions.

Shun as the adder in your path
   The tippler's hissing tankard,
Commixed with want, crime, ruin, death—
'Tis Satan's vial of fiendish wrath
   Poured out upon the drunkard!

Is in your breast " the softer flame ?"
   Well, see you rightly place it
On her of modest worthy fame,
Not on the flirt.   Oh, brand your name
   Never with love illicit.

And lassies, there 's a word or twa
   Of counsel due to you
Here wi' us, and frae hame awa',
Where Yankee gals look smart and braw,
   And sae you must be too.

Eydant wi' thrift, gie pride nae place;
   Live as becomes your station;
At fashion's gew-gaws mak' a face,
Knowing that plenty, health, and peace
   Are handmaids of discretion.

You 're weel disposed, and, to be win—
   Dread fell dissembler's art.
Remember you 've a foe within,
To virtue very near akin—
   A loving, yielding heart.

We 'll say naught now to mak' you blush
 Anent grave matrimony ;
But as it gets some into fash,
We beg ye not to be too rash—
 You 're yet beth young and bonny.

GALCACUS'S ADDRESS.

READ BEFORE THE ST. ANDREW'S SOCIETY.

Heroes of the unconquered North!
Caledonians, free by birth!
Now 's the hour to test your worth,
   Routing Roman bravery.

Celtic chieftain, ever brave,
Never can be branded slave!
His is freedom, or the grave;
   Hail, then, death or liberty!

Is renowned the Roman name?
Has Agricola matchless fame?
Well—to win this day the game
   Sure is worth our rivalry.

Shall the gleam of arms abash?
On the invaders let us rush!
Lightning like, our swords shall flash
   Through their shields of heraldry!

Raging seas round rocky shore—
Foaming cataracts—mountains hoar—
Woods of oak, and mines of ore,
   Stamp us free eternally !

Shall our bosom's martial glow
Then be quelled by any foe ?
Hark ! the Grampians echo " NO !"
   Forward ! on to victory !

See ! before this plundering host
Sacred homes their comfort boast !
Look ! behind it all is lost—
   Ruin, rapine, slavery !

Here, its eagle flight repel ;
Here, its mad ambition quell ;
Here, let deeds of valor tell
   Bounds to Roman robbery !

Let our parents feeble, old,
Wives exposed to violence bold,
Children into bondage sold,
   Rouse to feats of chivalry !

Hovering dreadful o'er our heads,
Are our famed forefathers' shades,
Witnessing the glorious deeds
   Of their true posterity !

If our sires have left us free,
Free our sons shall also be !
Latest times shall Scotchmen see
    Freemen like their ancestry !

Tho' a world to Rome should fall—
Servile bent beneath her thrall,
Caledonia never shall !
    She 's above her tyranny !

SONG.

"UP! CLANS OF OLD SCOTLAND," OR A CALL ON RESIDENT SCOTCH-
MEN TO JOIN THE ST. ANDREW'S SOCIETY.

Up! Clans of Old Scotland, let 's on to the fray;
Wi' beacons the hills are in blazing array!
Our countrymen coming, all friendless and roaming,
Ask of us bemoaning relief on their way;
While heard in our midst is the suppliant cry
Of the indigent widow and fatherless boy.
Wake! chiefs of the heather, and strike a' together!
In the field of benevolence great is the joy!

They come from the Highlands and glens of the North,
In plaid, kilt, and tartan, all chieftains of worth;
They come frae the Lowlan's, brought up in their hallins;
Richt auldfarren callans frae Tay, Tweed, and Forth,
Frae Clydesdale, and Nithsdale, and Annandale too,
Are farmers, mechanics, and artizans true;
Nor is there awanting, while feasting and chanting,
The pibroch's "Hurra for the bonnets o' blue."

To support their guid cause, all devoted and leal,
As Scotchmen united—as Scotchmen to feel.
But why are the ithers of clansmen and brithers,
Wha claim the same fathers, not with us for weal?
Come join, fellow-countrymen! national pride
And honor demands that you lend us your aid.
To stand at a distance, withholding assistance,
Of Scotchmen true born let it never be said!

How cheering to meet as a Yankee-Scotch clan
At the feast of our Saint, all agreed to a man!
And naething distressing, wi' charity's blessing,
Our lassies caressing, talk of our own lan'!
Of its mountains of heather and gowany braes;
Of its dells, where in childhood we rambled for slaes;
Of its bannocks, its bonnets, its science, its sonnets,
Its fairies, its heroes, its ALL!—if you please.

SONG FOR ST. ANDREW'S DAY.

AIR—"AULD LANG SYNE."

Should auld acquaintance be forgot,
    When thus we meet to dine?
Should Scotland dear be out o' thought,
    And days o' lang syne?
CHORUS—O! auld lang syne, my boys,
            O! auld lang syne
                We 'll balance wi' our present joys,
                And sing o' lang syne.

Tho' far awa' on distant shores,
    Yet fresh are in our min'
Her hills and dales, her glens and moors,
    And days o' lang syne.

Nae mair to us the laverock chaunts,
    And braes wi' gowans shine;
Nae mair we rove the sacred haunts
    O' youth and love lang syne.

Much that is dear behind is left,
　Yet let us ne'er repine;
Here, canty met, we hae the gift
　To—sing o' lang syne.

Should, in these woods, a brither Scot
　Himsel' be like to tyne,
We 'll set him right, and gie 'm a groat,
　For days o' lang syne.

And while we hail Columbia vast
　Now as our hame, sae fine,
We 'll still remember to our last
　Dear Scotia and lang syne.

BURNS ANNIVERSARY, 1849.

A CANTATA.

RECITATIVO.

On Erie's shelving, sandy beach,
Where, like a regal city, rich,
  Shine Cleveland's gilded spires,
A band of social fellows met,
In purpose high to celebrate
  Upon their new-strung lyres
The birthday of the Scottish bard,
  The famous Robert Burns;
And, that each one might strike a chord,
  All gave their song in turns.
    So rising, rejoicing
      As chief of all the clan,
    The chairman—a rare one—
    The opening lay began.

AIR.

The wheels of time have made their ninetieth turn
Since on the banks of Doon our bard was born;

Bleak penury, and humble toils and cares
Did mark his birth and all his early years.
No college classes trained his rising thought:
To hold the plow, 't was his sequestered lot.
"The softer flame" he felt, and then, to tell,
The muse was wooed to sing his "Handsome Nell."
Amidst his rural walks some lassie fair
Attracts—he sings her charms—surpassing rare.
Another's met—anon, his soul on flame,
He strikes his lyre and gives her lasting fame.
Hence, to his country—to the world belongs
The happiest—best of love-impassioned songs.
"Mary in Heaven" is (nor is this too bold)
Worthy the seraph and his harp of gold!
    In satire, humor, or sarcastic wit,
High stands his fame, if not unequaled yet,
As "Tam O'Shanter," "Hornbook," and "the Pair,"*
With other poems just as bright, declare.
    For the pathetic "bosom-melting throe,"
For patriotic sentimental glow,
For fine description of the rural scene,
In natural, extemporaneous strain,
"The Cotter's Night," "The Daisy," "The Lament,"
And "Scots wha hae" fall short of naught extant.
    Nor does our bard excel in verse alone:
His prose is such as would secure renown;

---

* The Twa Dogs.

His varied " Letters "—every one—are fraught
With bold originality of thought
Expressed with aptitude, with strength, with ease,
Alike to strike the fancy or the judgment please.

  Still his chief forte was conversational powers,
Which magic-like charmed all the social hours.
Hence, courted was his talk, and hence, alas!
The drunk carousal, fatal to his peace!
  —————————O ill-requited bard!
How true " on life's rough ocean luckless starred,"
By " thoughtless follies" prematurely urned;
Living, neglected; dead, with honors mourned.
Would thou hadst lived in this our Freedom's day,
When sense and worth laugh at imperial sway,
To sing, despite aristocrat control,*
"A man 's a man " of independent soul.

  *   *   *   *   *

But it appears in us presumption strong,
Here to descant on the famed Chief of Song.
The subject 's far above our feeble power—
With kindred feelings let us then adore.
The learned world, since death his harp unstrung,
Have vied to ape and eulogize his song.

---

  * Burns was more than once, by the Commissioners of the Excise
impeached as a political offender—a democrat. Being once in a large com-
pany, " The health of Wm. Pitt" was proposed. Burns vehemently demur-
red against it, and wished to substitute " The health of a greater and better
man, Geo. Washington." This being rejected, he immediately left the house
in great indignation.—[See Lockhart's Edition of Burns.]

Auld Scotia erst was great in sterling worth,
But it took Burns to set her virtues forth—
To give to deathless fame her rural scenes—
Her braes, her mountains, rivers, woods, and glens—
To sanctify in song the cotter's cot—
His loves, his joys, his griefs, his every lot.
Those of us Scotch, of him may truly boast,
Whose genius honors on a foreign coast.
Many a noble form the "tuneful band,"
Both of our native and adopted land,
And place pre-eminent claims on our shelf;
Yet Burns is Scotland—and a Scotchman's self.
What tho' no sculptured monument may rise
Here to his fame, and meet admiring eyes,
Still, does not this assembly declare
In prouder marks—he lives in memory dear?
The marble obelisk, the regal throne,
Will sink to dust forgotten and unknown;
But Burns shall live while freedom, song, and love
Glow in the human breast enkindled from above.

RECITATIVO.

He paused.   And now the goblet crown'd
   "Unto the memory of the dead,"
Did pass the standing vot'ries round;
   Meanwhile, as if the immortal shade
Was present and beheld the scene,
   "Expressive silence mused," and awe profound did reign.

Anon, the Chair, 'Squire Robie Parks,
    Before he took his seat,
In a few pertinent remarks
    Upon the cause, why met,
Gave all a cordial invitation
To take a part on the occasion.

Nearest akin unto the bard,
    The Scotch had called the meeting;
Yet each, and all, without regard,
    Did justly claim a greeting:
For who is there, gay, grave, or learned,
In Colia's poet not concerned?

So Patrick, from the Emerald Isle,
Stepped forth, and gave in native style
    This song.   He had composed it
Just ere he left his native soil,
To cheer him on through unknown toil
    When love of home opposed it;
And now that Fortune had proved kind,
The grateful feelings of his mind
    Spontaneously proposed it.

AIR.

Och! why live I here to dull drudgery tame,
    The sad child of scorn, want, and care,
When competence, ease, independence, and fame
    Invite to Ohio the fair?

Too long like a slave for the proud have I toiled—
  For what?—Och! I blush to declare!
Half-fed and half-clad and half-starved have I moiled;
  But no more—for Ohio the fair.

Dear! dear to my soul is the hall of my fathers—
  The scenes of my childhood, how dear!
But then how to get a bare living so pothers—
  I go—to Ohio the fair.

To me, on the banks of the Shannon, no more
  The shamrock scents sweetly the air.
I brandish the axe in the woods evermore—
  Hail! hail to Ohio the fair!

Ye friends of my youth! fellow drudges, farewell!
  No longer your hardships I share.
My *all* for a passage! one effort shall tell
  I 'm a man in Ohio the fair!

RECITATIVO.

Attention! Bell now takes the floor,
An " O'er-the-March-elopement-splore,"
In which a striking part he bore,
    He sings wi' glee.
It happened just twa days before
    He crossed the sea.

10

AIR—A SERENADE.

TUNE: "*Jock o' Hazeldeen.*"

Ho! sleeps my lady! ho! awake!
　　Awake and dress thee gay!
Thy Willie 'neath thy window waits
　　To bear thee sly away.
Twa Arabs fleet stand ready by,
　　Escort to Gretna-Green;
It is thy lover's weel ken'd sigh!
　　Make haste, my lovely Jean.

The plashing mill-wheel darkly rests,
　　The anvil's din is still,
The hamlet 's sunk in deepest sleep—
　　All things just to our will!
The very dog of watchfu' bark
　　Mars not the silent scene;
Nae e'e our secret flight shall mark—
　　Sae haste thee, dearest Jean.

Out o'er the Bank the lovely moon,
　　And Venus by her side,
Seem shining only thee t' invite
　　To rise and be my bride.
The lamps of night wi' joyous beam
　　Light all the way serene:
For love and thee heaven's torches flame—
　　Sae come, my charming Jean.

Thy worthy aunt—now rest her saul—
　Bequeathed to thee her wealth ;
And would a spendthrift daddie rob
　Thee of it all by stealth ?
Hark ! now he snores—be brave ! elope !
　Nor dread his after spleen.
With love what passion yet could cope ?
　O haste, my fairest Jean.

Thou can'st not doubt my love, my truth,
　My honor, or my aim ;
Nor think, if resting on thy couch,
　That this is all a dream !—
She comes ! O, raptures ! art thou mine ?
　Drop in my arms, my queen !
Now, on ye steeds, to Hymen's shrine !
　You bear my peerless Jean !

RECITATIVO.

Lawyer Tam, from Mona's* strand
Did attention next command.
Plaintive was his voice and strain—
Feelings given to his pen,
When, of every joy bereft,
His beloved home he left.

---

* The Isle of Man.

Tune: "*Ye Banks and Braes o' Bonnie Doon.*"

Returning Spring unfolds again
   Its vernal joys, oft hailed with glee,
But sadness now pervades each scene;
   Stern fate compels across the sea!
Tho' I may mark on distant shore
   Spring's beauties new and varied smile,
Yet such will lack, to cheer, the power
   Here felt in this my native isle.

Let me away, ere blows the bud
   Of flowery mead and gowany lea,
Where oft in youth's gay spring I 've trod,
   Not dreaming I 'd to cross the sea;
Nor waft, ye playful breezes, round
   The scent of hawthorn bloom, the while,
To pierce the soul with blissful wound—
   I leave you, and my native isle.

Suspend, sweet lark, thy soaring note;
   Thou chaunt'st a farewell hymn to me:
O, shall I find a tuneful throat
   To cheer like thine across the sea!
Thou gentle stream that wanders by,
   Dost thou in murmurs soft revile,
And speak of every youthful joy,
   On leaving now my native isle?

Adieu, sweet cottage of my birth,
   How curls thy smoke so gracefully ;
All that is dear to me on earth,
   Is left in thee to cross the sea.
Delightful Eden ! let us part !
   The cause—well, I was void of guile—
Would I had lack'd this feeling heart !
   I must—must leave my native isle !

RECITATIVO.

He ended : less was the applause
Than Yankee-guessing what the cause
He left for—Hark ye, sirs ! it was
    (Yet don't be talking)
One moonlit night, against the laws,
    He shot a—maukin.*

But hush ! a song from Sandy Patton :
His lassie had gie'n him the mitten ;
So he embarked straight, no one witting,
    To vex the jilt,
And now with Yankee gal 'gain smitten,
    He raised his lilt.

AIR.
TUNE: "*Corn Rigs are Bonnie.*"

One summer night as I did stroll
   Along the banks of Erie,
I chanced to meet a Yankee gal—
   Her name, another Mary.

---

* Hare.

The waters rippling kissed the shore;
　The moon was shining clearly;
The woods entwined an amorous bower
　And all for me and Mary.

To queens of other lands I 've knelt,
　Adoring most sincerely;
But cold were all my raptures felt
　Compared to these with Mary!
Her seraph form, her heavenly eye,
　Her lips the sweetest cherry;
Her gracious whisper to my sigh—
　All that I wished was Mary!

And now my wife, with children two,
　Content we live and cheerie;
In thrift, in sense, in virtue too
　Domestic shines my Mary.
Then let each lad his lassie keep;
　I envy not his dearie,
Since earth's supremest bliss I reap
　In wedlock with my Mary!

CHORUS.

Scotch lochs and Yankee lakes
　Beat creation fairly;
But fair or grand in either land
　There 's none like lovely Erie!

RECITATIVO.

The next in order now before us
Is one who joined not the last chorus—
   It was a sweeping strophie :
A hick'ry nut within his cheek
Harder to chew than acrid leek,
   The symbol of St. Taffy.
The fact is this : He had hither come
   In buoyant expectation
To make within a year a plum
   And fill some lofty station ;
      But foiled here and broiled here,
      He found he could not cope
   With spunkies of Yankees ;
      So thus, forsook by hope :

AIR.

Tune: "*Loch-na-gar.*"

Away with your lakes that like so many oceans,
   Surrounded with forests, roll savage and drear !
Away with your gals and your strange Yankee notions !
   Restore me St. Winefrid's Well ever clear !
They told me, when holding the plough of my father,
   That here for the lifting were dollars in store ;
So big with the hopes that a million I 'd gather,
   I left, sailed, and landed on Lake Erie shore.

O Avarice! thou cursed, infernal allurer!
  O Fortune! thou fickle, capricious jade!
Here shaven—here skinned—every day I get poorer!
  There 's nothing but barter, and orders, and trade!
O had I the joys of the jolly Welsh farmer
  Attending his herds on the grand Penman mawr,
Or turning the furrow by Dee's gentle murmur,
  Ne'er again would I be upon Lake Erie's shore!

RECITATIVO.

Here Whitelaw's pity did awaken,
So moved that measures should be taken
To soothe him in his exile pain,
Or ship him o'er the seas again.
But self-important Johnny Bull
Grown quite the Yankee at free school,
  Cried, "Go ahead, ye negro!"
And without farther of preamble
Struck up his recent sparkling ramble
  In solo, brisk allegro.

AIR.
TUNE: "*Yankee Doodle.*"

Some fifteen years ago, a boy
  Hailed this shore of Erie;
All was strange to ear and eye,
  But his heart was merry.
    Yankee doodle, Yankee dee,
      Thrift will stamp ye lucky;
    By my Ann, anr I the one!
    Yankee doodle, Buckeye.

One in England left behind—
  Playmate of his childhood—
Ever present in his mind,
  Cheered the toils of wildwood.
    Yankee doodle, etc.

Oft by Avon's classic tide
  The rushy wreath he 'd wove her,
And with her culled the flowers, and played
  The child and artless lover.
    Yankee doodle, etc.

To defend from seeming harm
  His arm was thrown around her,
And why their bosoms beat so warm
  'T was then to both a wonder.
    Yankee doodle, etc.

Again to see her home he hied,
  While love the steamer paddle
Chid as slow, and wished to stride
  A telegraphic saddle.
    Yankee doodle, etc.

Home he reaches—finds his Ann
  Awaiting him, true hearted:
Banns are cried—and they made one
  Till death—not seas them parted.
    Yankee doodle, etc.

Soon is bid a last good-bye
   To the scenes of childhood;
To Ohio back they hie,
   Hailing glad the wildwood.
     Yankee doodle, etc.

Who the homestead would forego,
   Nobly independent,
For the lordling's haughty no!
   Servilely attendant?
     Yankee doodle, Yankee done!
      Ne'er was man so lucky!
     By my Ann, am I the one?
      Yankee doodle, Buckeye!

RECITATIVO.

Now Jonathan doth grace the floor—
A noble fellow at the core—
Of wealth, in Cleveland none had more,
   Nor better used it.
Through Europe, when on a late tour
   His song he 'd mused it.

AIR.

TUNE: "*My Heart 's in the Highlands.*"

My heart 's in Ohio, my heart is not here;
My heart 's in Ohio with Lucy, my dear;
With Lucy, my dear, at my sweet native home—
My heart 's in Ohio wherever I roam.

To finish my learning they 've hit on a plan—
To polish my taste and accomplish the man
Afar I must travel, but what for, my love?
Ah, Lucy! thy charms, and they only, improve.

Care I for the beauties of fable to trace—
The paintings of Rome, or the statues of Greece?
Such please not my taste, nor my fancy enthrall—
Fair Lucy, my Venus, surpasses them all!

Proud England may boast of her sweet blushing rose,
And France in gay fashion her lily disclose—
They warm not, they charm not like Lucy, my fair;
She—she is the queen of her sex everywhere!

My Lucy 's the dearest! and what makes her so?
Her bosom 's the lily, her eye is the sloe,
Her mind is the fane of love, virtue, and peace;
True merit attendant and each smiling grace.

Then blame not my heart, while I wander afar,
In being with Lucy, my bright polar star.
Attractions she hath that allure me to home
And cheer me and steer me wherever I roam.

RECITATIVO.

Young Stuart follows: In a grove
  Round which Cuyahoga bent there,
A pretty, gentle, amorous dove
  Had made his heart to pant there.

So stranger to th' illicit rove
    Or passion's wild adventure,
Inspired by youthful hope and love
    He blows aloud his chanter
        T' her praise that night.

AIR.

TUNE: *"Dumbarton's Bonny Belle."*

Of all the rivers east or west
    Which Yankeedom doth tell,
To me Cuyahoga is the best—
    Fair Betsy there doth dwell.
In mind ánd person formed complete,
    There 's none doth her excel;
'Bove vulgar praise, accomplished, sweet,
    She 's Cuyahoga's lovely belle.

Proud Mississippi's sweeping tide,
    Niagara's mighty swell,
Delight not like Cuyahoga's glide
    Meandering thro' the dell.
It has a gem of worth untold—
    A treasure nonpareil;
Not Sacramento's bed of gold
    Could buy Cuyahoga's belle.

Flow on, thou gentle river, flow,
    Till heard is Time's own knell,
Famed for the patriotic beau
    And home-endearing belle.

But quickly come thou day divine,
    When twenty-one shall tell
That Betsy is forever mine—
    Cuyahoga's lovely belle.

RECITATIVO.

Next Edwin, frae auld Reekie City—
    A queer auld-fashioned carl—
Proposed to gie his favorite ditty,
    "The thrifty spinning girl!"
Both sang and tune he thought were pretty,
    Aye, worth the richest pearl!
And like some ither, to seem witty,
    Fancied grimace and skirl
            Best ony night.

AIR.

Let proud aspiring beaux address
    The belle o' high degree;
Let dandy fops gallant the lass
    That 's glaiket, braw, and spree;
Let warl'y coofs gie court the toast,
    And for a tocher kneel;
But gie to me the thrifty maid
    Wha busy twirls the wheel.

The prim-mouth'd-prude, the flippant flirt,
    The gaudy butterfly,
Ken naething how to shape a shirt
    Or hush a babie's cry.

They dreaming lie till noon in bed,
  Then at the glass look weel
For evening ball or masquerade,
  A' strangers to the wheel.

Our gentle folks extol the dame
  That on pianos drum,
But she 's the ane to cheer my hame
  Wha on the wheel doth bumm.
The mansion gran', the silken dress,
  May sometimes wealth reveal;
But the sign o' plenty, health, and peace
  Is the bumm of the spinning wheel.

Wae 's me! for puir or rich that 's gat
  A wife wha canna' spin,
For factory duds, I weel-a-wat!
  To nane are near akin.
There 's naething beats the hame-spun coat
  For tear and wear and biel;
Sae let that man ay bliss his lot
  Whase wife can twirl the wheel.

In Proverbs, chapter last, we read,
  Where a guid wife 's the sang,
That she is ane wha spins a thread—
  Makes webs beth fine and lang:

Her auld guid-man 's kenned by his plaid;
　Her bairns gang sarkit weel—
Sae gie to me the thrifty maid
　Wha busy twirls the wheel.

RECITATIVO.

Here Mac cried "Order," thinking that
The song was far frae being pat.
"We 're met this night," he blabbed out,
　"To ca' the crack, not wi' a *rockin'*—
To crack of Burns, not rave about
Spinning wheels, now obsolete,
　Sic hodden stuff provokin'.
Cameron, frae St. Andrew's College,
　Wants to speak, (and he 's auldfarran,)
While he lacks not classic knowledge,
Scottish legendary lore
He hath in store,
　So I move he gets a hearing."

Cameron, called on, made his bow—
Told his tale quite apropos;
Followed quickly by another,
And another merry-meeting-making brother;
But as the fun grew "fast and furious,"
The scribbler-Bard, like Tam O'Shanter,
Tickled with the sport so glorious,
Quite forgot
To make a note,

And so now he dare na' venture
To try the same
Sae far frae hame,
Upon an Indian chanter.
    The following stanzas,
    Amid his fancies,
    However he did min',
    In which joined all
    Within the hall,
    As in days o' lang syne.

AIR.

TUNE: "*Auld Lang Syne.*"

Should native Scotland, land o' cakes,
    Be never brought to min',
When, in the land o' Johnnie cakes,
    We meet to crack or dine?

CHORUS.

The Thistle bloom, how fine, my friends;
    The Buckeye shade, how fine!
So ere we part let 's drink to beth,
    And days o' lang syne.

Oft hae the linnet, lark, and thrush
    Delighted wi' their strain;
Now hoop-o-will and mocking-bird
    Please wi' their comic vein.

The channelstane we ance did thraw
  And had diversions prime;
Now over crisping wreaths o' snaw
  The sleigh-bells merry chime.

From heather hills and gowany braes
  We 've viewed the oat-clad plain;
Now, lost midst stretching lawns of maize,
  The melon's juice we drain.

At wedding, tryst, or kirn we had
  Rare daffin' wi' our Jeans;
At quiltings now and paring-bees
  We spark our Yankee queens.

Then why should we, my jovial boys,
  At change o' lot repine?
The present, wi' its cares, hae joys
  Like days o' lang syne.

———

Thus past the hours in free exchange
Of speech, of song, and story strange
  Until the clock struck one,
Admonishing now in her turn
Our social fellows to adjourn
  And close that night their fun;

11

So when a motion had been ta'en
  That how the night was spent
Should by the Bardie's Doric pen
  Be scribbled out to print,
All parted and started
  For hame their "several way,"
Dissolved, resolved
  "To meet some ither day."

THE ANNIVERSARY OF BURNS, 1855.

———

Just as it ought to be—all social, hearty,
Distinction none of nation, sect, or party.
Auld Caledonia gave the Plow-boy birth,
But Genius stampt him Bard for the whole earth.
So be it known, to all whom it concerns,
This is the Anniversary of Burns.

My Brother Jonathan! you laugh at kings—
At belted knights and all their gew-gaw things;
And in the spirit of Democracy
Would worship at the shrine of Liberty
As all the patriot in your bosom burns—
Weel, such-like Yankee notions kindled Burns.

My "gentler sister," woman! yes, you know
That you 're Creation's crowning work below;
But "let me whisper in your lug" refined,
Not half your charms of person or of mind—
Of loveliness and goodness which adorns—
Had e'er been told, save by the lyre of Burns.

Ye who " for honest poverty's " abash'd,
Or ye who 'neath oppression's rod are crushed,
Think on the " Bard of independent wish,"
Who laughed at rank and all its tinsel trash.
"A man 's a man "—tho' Fortune frowning spurns—
That 's " got the pith of sense and worth " like Burns.

Ye prudes of Virtue and ye critics wise,
Spare now your cant and dare to criticize:
The lapse of years but vindicates his fame,
Wide as the world resounds his honest name,
And last it shall while earth " diurnal turns "—
Time's mighty ages are the years of Burns.

Ye boys of fun, of humor, wit, and cheer,
And ye who give to human woes a tear;
Ye Nature's votaries; ye who admire
The scenes of Scotia, and her lovely lyre—
Come one and all, till " the short hour " adjourns,
And, as true brothers, feel at home with Burns.

THE VISION.

———

READ AT THE BURNS FESTIVAL, 1857.

———

Instead of sleep, to take the air
And banish for a while dull care,
The other night our Public Square
     Of many a rood,
Did find me strolling here and there
     In musing mood.

The city's lamps around did burn,
And heavens above all taciturn;
While sleepy-like, pale, and forlorn,
     On Erie's breast
Sighing, the moon with crescent horn
     Sank to her rest.

The Second's and the Plymouth's tower
Had tolled aloud night's irksome hour
With more than mechanism's power,
  When 'fore my nose,
Hard by our fountain's jetty shower,
  A figure rose.

Wow! but it put me in a swat—
The bristling hair did lift my hat,
My very heart played pit-a-pat,
  And breathing stopt,
While frae my mouth agape, "What 's that?"
  Unconscious dropt.

But as the Four* burned magic bright,
I soon recovered frae my fright
And recognized, wi' great delight,
  One near akin.
(We bards that hae the second sight
  Have curious een.)

'T was symmetry itself—the form
Of female beauty, grace, and charm;
The features blythe, expressive, warm,
  Bespoke a heart
Fitted alike for war's fierce storm
  Or peaceful art.

---

* Lamps placed around the fountain.

Wild flowers and blossoms o' the thorn
Her auburn tresses did adorn,
While o'er her shoulder, with a turn
    Quite independent,
Her robe, streaked like the dawn of morn,
    Shone all transcendent !

Drawn on its opening folds, the eye
With pleasing wonder could descry
Our city and its destiny
    In times to come.
How glorious ! 'bove conception high,
    Our children's home.

There, as a centre, shone " the Square,"
With rural fountain, fresh and fair ;
Frae dingy city's dust and care,
    A haunt how blest !
Nae oasis delightful mair
    On Afric waste.

There grave Cuyahoga frae the woods
Lake Erie welcomes ; on their floods
Rides commerce brisk ; from factories, clouds
    Of steam ascend ;
While far-linked trains converging roads
    Together blend.

On this, its upper fringe of green,
Wharves, crammed with shipping, could be seen;
On that, and interspersed between,
      Rose school and college
And princely dome, in all the sheen
        Of rural foliage.

But time not half was there to trace
The beauties of her flowing dress,
Or mark the features of her face
      Divinely sweet,
Till she, with a young mother's grace,
        Did thus me greet:

"All hail, my son! I 'm glad to meet thee,
And as thy muse adopted greet thee;
The subject of thy proposed ditty
      Must tell my fame;
For I the genius of this city
        Myself proclaim.

"So take this harp and try thy hand
First on the Square," she said, quite bland:
I took the harp—she raised her wand,
      And lo! there shone
The Square—as in its future, grand!
        But she was gone!

And the old court house is no longer found
A legal trespasser on the public ground ;
Nor intersecting street of dirt and dust,
Nor clumsy fence the stranger to disgust,
No other nuisance—all had given place
To scenes of grandeur, love, utility, and grace.

CURLIANA.

READ BEFORE THE BURNS CURLING CLUB, 1858.

While famed bardies tune the harp
　　And of battles sing, most dire,
Just let us essay to chirp,
　　On our half-strang rustic lyre,
The contested, bright champaign of a spiel—
　　Our auld country's sport, sae nice—
　　A pitched game upon the ice,
　　And away wi' cards and dice
　　　　To the de'il !

When bleak winter rules the year
　　Wi' his nipping rod of frost,
Till the plow of polished share
　　In the hardened soil doth rust ;
Every river, loch, and pond frozen o'er ;
　　Then our Curlers may be seen
　　In their native pride, I ween,
　　Meeting on some ice that 's keen—
　　　　A blythe corps.

Heroes of the tramp and broom!
   When you marshal for "the game,"
If you 've never learned to swoom,
   Choose the meadow-burnie's dam—
Not the bottomless and wide-stretching lake.
   How appalling! just to think!
   Midst the crashing, yawning chink
   One and all at once to sink!
      Mercy's sake!

Soon the *rink* is sacred ground:
   Distant fifty yards are seen
The twa *whittees* circled round,
   With the sad *hog-score* between.
And now hark! "The game 's begun," bawls each *skip.*
   "Here a *lead,* be gently starr'd "—
   "Cannie, steady, lie a *guard* "—
   "Where 's your thunder? hit him hard!"
      "Let him rip!"

Sandy rests upon the *cock*;
   Davie skillfu' *wicks the bore;*
Jock gies an electric shock,
   Sending Tam and Will ashore;
While young Jemmie lags a *hog!* "Swoop him up!"
   Bravo! Rab 's a stirring bairn!
   And our Sam 's a roaring Quairn!
   But wi' Harry's stubborn airn
      Wha can cope?

As contending fleets at sea
  Mingle in the dreadful fray,
So the stanes reel round the *tee,*
  Quartered close in dexter play.
As if empires were at stake strive they all.
  To the trout wha eyes *incog.*
  All this jostle, pomp, and vogue,
  What a funny forkit frog
      Man must sprawl !

Had Dame Nature in her head
  This our Curliana fun,
When the comets vast she made,
  Launching them frae sun to sun,
Making besoms of the streamers for the Powers ?
  Yes ; ye brave Scotch-Yankee boys,
  Pitch your marbles and rejoice,
  For the Bonspiel's nobler joys
      All are yours !

Scotchmen ! when you rally out
  By Cuyahoga's winding stream,
Waking Echo wi' the shout
  Of your fathers' " roaring game,"
See you let her ne'er repeat aught of shame !
  While you cherish social mirth
  In the field or round the hearth,
  Let your deeds all speak of worth,
      Love, and fame.

On the slippery *rink* of life
  We have all to play a part ;
Let us then into the strife
  With a valiant hand and heart ;
Our antagonists are arch, skilled, and vast.
  Looking always at our card,
  Let us *chap, in ring,* or *guard*
  So that ours be the reward
    At the last.

THE BURNS CENTENARY.

READ BEFORE THE CALEDONIAN ASSOCIATION, 1859.

To celebrate our Burns' birth-day
Of late there has been great assay,
And may not we, for school-boy play
            Attempt to show it—
Tho' Scotch by birth, yet by his lay
            He 's mankind's poet.

A hundred years hae ta'en their flight,
Last Januar's five and twentieth night,
Since Robin first did see the light
            In th' auld clay biggin',
The hansel win's wi' raving flyte
            Tirlin' the riggin'.

Some eighty years or more have fled
Since he commenced the rhyming trade;
And many a bard has crazed his head
　　　In hopes to peer him,
But fient ane yet hae tuned the reed
　　　As to come near him.

His lear—a' that he did desire—
Was just a spark o' nature's fire;
The mother wit struck from his lyre
　　　Seemed as if given
To cheer the drudge thro' dub and mire—
　　　A light from heaven.

As he hath sang: He was a bard
On life's rough ocean luckless starr'd;
Devoid of aim—misfortune hard
　　　Did on him press;
While thoughtless follies often marr'd
　　　His inward peace.

His ae wee faut, or maybe twa,
O'er which the "unco guid" did craw,
Seemed in the balance nought ava
　　　To his rare gift,
Which gied his country—mankind a'—
　　　A wonder lift.

And then, besides his glorious parts,
Say mankind were a pack o' carts
He was the king—the ace o' hearts,
　　　True, honest, warm,
That gave to all of his deserts
　　　　Their native charm.

He liked the lassies—that is true !
But lassies, that was good for you :
His songs, your beauties (not a few)
　　　Set a' abreed ;
And gied the heart o' laithfu' beau
　　　　An unco screed.

Albeit it was his darling theme
Sweetly to chant "the softer flame,"
Yet Freedom's patriotic name
　　　Firing his breast
Enrich'd the world wi' mony a gem
　　　　Not yet surpassed.

His humor charmed the social hour
And set the table in a roar ;
While his sarcastic wit did scour
　　　Like any grunstane !
Woe to the victim !—'t was a show'r
　　　　Of fire and brunstane.

Were mirth and fun his cronies dear,
Woe also had his pitying tear;
The tim'rous mouse, the wounded hare,
   His yowe, poor Mailie,
The happin' bird in winter drear
   A' had his wailie.

Wha wad na fill his comrade's grave,
To live in elegiac stave
The friend beloved, true, gen'rous, brave?
   At others' woe,
All sensitive, his heart did heave
   In melting throe!

His creed:—being nae sectarian rant
He made a deevil o' the saint
Whose prayers were hypocritic cant
   For self-promotion.
Has his "Let's worship God" a want
   Of true devotion?

That man 's a man, friend, husband, brother;
That woman 's sister, wife, and mother;
Ay, every tie that binds together
   The human race.
Has he not sung—or nature rather—
   With truth and grace?

12

His rustic reed—his pen a grissle—
His crambo-clink—his prose epistle,
Telling of Scotland and her thistle,
   Doth mair than swords
To blast fell tyrants, or the whistle
   Of haughty lords!

Tho' humble was our Poet's birth,
And life the life of suffering worth,
Unsheltered fra ill's biting north,
   Yet deathless fame
To the remotest nook of earth
   Blazons his name.

Morn's lingering star shall cease to glow,
Heather on Scotland's hills to blow,
Afton and bonny Doon to flow,
   And love to cherish,
Ere Burns's fame decay shall know,
   Or fail to flourish.

ROBBIE BURNS.

READ BEFORE THE CLEVELAND CURLING CLUB, 1861.

Ye Cleveland Curliana chiels !
Brave heroes of a hundred spiels !
As Time ance mair on rapid wheels
      Your Day returns,
Permit, fra ane that wi' you feels,
      A verse on Burns.

To keep alive the patriot flame—
Associations fond of hame—
You here pursue your favorite game,
      And taste the joy o't
Beneath the ægis of the name
      Of Scotland's Poet.

Along the shore of Yankee lakes
Enchanted rise the Land o' Cakes ;
Echo, as if delighted, wakes
   And re-rehearses
The dialect a Curler speaks,
    And Burns's verses.

Weel, here in these your Winters hoary,
See that you mak' life's pleasant story
Read like your fathers' pristine glory,
   Setting meanwhile
As an example bright before ye
    The lad o' Kyle.

Does Poortith or dame Fortune crush
Your spirit's "independent wish,"
And to a cipher damn your cash
   On merchant's ledger?
Cheer up! for such did sadly lash
    Puir Burns the Gauger.

When Love's pulsation madd'ning warms,
And lassies wi' their witching charms
Lure you to catch them in your arms,
   Their bosoms throbbin',
Think how the Session raised alarms—
    Cutty-stool'd Robin.

And see, my friends, you bear in mind
"When e'er to drink you are inclined,"
That wives at home await you kind
        And prattling bairns;
O be to this not deaf nor blind!
        Remember Burns!

And let "the rattling boys" of fun—
The child of humor, wit, and pun—
Each "whim-inspired" Muse's son,
        Mark the reward:
Neglect did shroud the setting sun
        O' Nature's Bard.

If fired with the poetic flame,
A swerving wight devoid of aim,
You pant to gain a deathless name,
        Blowing the chanter,
Use Nature's reed and you've the fame
        Of Rab the Ranter.

To keep your dignity of mind
With sensibility refined,
To be an honest, social, kind,
        Heroic, true man,
Before the eye as frontlet bind
        The Scottish ploughman.

And lassies!—sae far weel-behaved,
(Frae a' temptation be ye saved,)
Just hark ye!—not to be believed
      Is ilka chiel!
Were not some Mauchline belles deceived
      By Rab Mossgiel?

"Ye brethren o' the mystic tie,"
To rise in order grand and high,
The line and plummet walking by,
      Set not another
Before the hieroglyphic eye
      Than Burns your Brother.

That ye may lang these scenes revive,
And a' your Bardie's virtues drive,
His wee faut shunning—ever thrive—
      'S the pray'r sincerest
Of your puir representative
      O' mankind's rarest!

SCOTTISH GAMES.

———

THEIR INAUGURATION AT CLEVELAND, OHIO, SEPTEMBER 27, 1867. READ BEFORE THE BURNS CURLING CLUB, JANUARY 24, 1868.

———

O for a Pindar's famous lyre !
Or rather Tennant's humorous fire,
  To sing auld Scotia's sports ;
Their favorable inauguration,
Their first and happy celebration
By citizens of every nation
  In Cleveland's sweet resorts.

Of Nature's planting, there's a grove
  East of the city's dust and din,
Called Willson from its Scottish owner,
  The sacred haunt of youth and love—
    An Eden fair when without sin—
This was the field of contest, mirth, and honor.

As if participating the day's fun,
    The jocund Sun
      Looked laughingly out o'er the Shaker woods
      And crimson-fringed the clouds
      That coped the arena, and to which the roads
Were thronged with mony a man and mither's son.

The bird of passage sang his farewell solo ;
   The sere leaf of September crowned the bush ;
The squirrel peep'd from out his beech tree hollow
   At the invasion's most intrusive rush ;
The cause of such a scene, divine he could not,
So from his harvest store he cracked a hickory good nut.

A smooth, green flowery square enclosed with rope
Marked out the place of dext'rous feat and hope ;
Round the spectators crowded to behold ;
Some stood, some rode, some in their carriage rolled.
        While the airs of Papworth's band
        To suit the occasion grand
        Made Yankee Buckeye land
        Seem Caledonian strand.
  The flags of blue—of star and unicorn—
Blazoning the day, were high in the breeze upborne !

  Hark ! 't is the drum's attention-rattle,
    The games are to begin—
  Hush'd are the gathering's friendly tattle,
    The bustle and the din,

As now the herald of the day aloud
From mounted hillock thus addressed the crowd :

" My worthy frien's and countrymen !
   In the name of fun athletic—
Cheerer of youth's past-time hours—
   We have planted, all ecstatic,
Scotland's standard in these bowers
   That we may repeat again,
'Neath its flappings and its sheen,
Boyhood sports of meadow green.
   Tho' they 're Scotch—the exercises—
      Those of other countries may
   Freely combat for the prizes—
      Win the trophies of the day.
   Chosen judges, leal and true,
   Shall to merit give its due.
   True born heroes, enter then !
   First we try the putting-stane."

   He paused : ten chieftains stout and trig
      Within the ring arise ;
   They, poising high the ponderous craig,
      Hurl it thro' the skies.
   But Andrew's Jock strode o'er the rig
      And frae his arm it flies—
   A thunderbolt, that whizzing dug
      O'er a' their dints, the prize—
            Mighty that day !

A mile in length now starts the race—
 A score are on the roll—
Not lang abreast, but in a chase
 They strive wi' panting soul.
See! Clydesdale Wat and Nithsdale Case
 Ahead run cheek by jowl.
Ah! how they swallow up the space
 And straining pass the goal—
  Dead-heat that day!

Now come a squad o' barefit boys
 Like hounds let frae the slip;
Halloo! ahead Bill tak's all eyes,
 Sae nimble does he skip;
But at his heels Jim eager hies,
 His very panties rip!
Wow! heels over head Bill hapless flies,
 While glorying in his trip
  Jim gains the day.

Anither race! ho! clear the track!
 Ten live Egyptian mummies!
Each in a sack tied round the neck
 To go it—O, what nummies!
About the hurdle on their back
 They spurtle like bound lammies;
But tailor Rab wi' hop-flea knack
 Popped up and made the game his
  'Mid cheers that day!

Anither—a three-legged ane!
  In pairs, tied by the shanks,
They make a rather awkward rin,
  Like wheels that turn on cranks.
Tho' Tam and Sam puffed hard to win,
  It was their lot—twa blanks.
Brisk Jack and Gill passed skelping in—
  Why ?—'cause they both were Manx
        For legs that day.

Now comes the contest o' the loup,
  Beth in its length and height—
Standing—or wi' a ram race swoop,
  All wondrous in their flight!
Brave Rab the Bruce and Johnnie Coup
  Stood first best in their might;
While Simon landing on his doup
  I' the dirt, swore he was straight
        Wi' beth that day!

Does twal feet dyke put out o' reach
  Yon orchard's fruit sae mellow?
There 's Aleck wi' his vaulting crutch
  Can o'er it like a swallow!
Cuyahoga in its broadest stretch,
  When Boreas' billows bellow,·
Can bounded be fra beach to beach
  Or strode by sic a fallow
        Just ony day!

Now comes recess—a short ha'f hour—
　　Of interest great, I ween:
See! squads of sax to maist a score
　　Sit on the flowery green,
Blessing the basket and the store
　　Of lassies in their sheen.
O, sweet repast in love's own bower!
　　Sure ne'er the like has been
　　　　　　Since youth's-hame-day!

"Frien's," cries the herald, "to commence
　　Again the exercises
On the green sward we 'll hae a dance
　　In which all join wha pleases."—
Ye learned folks in Greek romance,
　　Your naiads, nymphs, and graces
Are but weird gypsies in a prance
　　Compared to these meek daisies,
　　　　　　In truth that day!

At "hitch and kick," (next feat we sing)
　　The best o' nine was Sandy;
He wi' his foot the bell did ring—
　　Height—fifteen feet—quite handy.
Sym said that he could kick the thing,
　　So he, the starched-up dandy,
In trial turned the wild-cat-fling
　　And skailed his pouchfu' candy
　　　　　　On the green that day!

With wheel-barrow to go it blind
   And box the post i' the center,
Some dozen had made up their mind
   To try it for the banter;
So make your mark and snuff the wind,
   Then for it in a canter.
Pshaw! lost and wandering!—all resigned!
   Save Ned, wha at a venture
         Bumped it that day!

Three pair prepared now ready stand
   For mastery in the wrestle,
A Rob Roy, William Wallace band,
   For stalwart bone and gristle!
Lang was the contest—eager, grand,
   The agonizing tussle!
But Mike at last the upper hand,
   By straining every muscle,
         Gat that proud day.

Now in the lake red sank the sun
   As hameward bodies wended,
Rehearsing pleased the day's rare fun:
   And so my epic 's ended.
But in despite of monk or nun,
   It really is intended
At Gymnic new to fire the gun
   And hae things far mair splendid
         Some after day.

Ye pious folks! on such-like spare
  Anathemic aspersion!
Body and mind demand repair
  When crushed by much exertion.
Best antidote for cankering care
  Is innocent diversion:
You 've got the blues?—O, don't despair!
  But gie them all dispersion
        Wi' the Scots some day!

AMERICAN CURLIANA.

READ BEFORE THE BURNS CURLING CLUB, 1869. AIR—"TULLOCH-
GORUM."

Again the day of Robert Burns
With this our festival returns,
Sae here 's to a' whom it concerns
  A song o' Curliana:
It is the game of games confessed ;
Game the fairest, game the rarest,
Game the dearest and the best,
   This game of Caledonia.
Gie feckless cit his parlor nice,
Billiards, gammon, cards, and dice,
But gie a Scotchman routh o' ice
   To drive his Curliana.

When Liberty, sweet goddess! came
Frae her own skies to seek a hame,
She sang, on spying curler-game,
   " My realm is Caledonia,
And curler-boys my sons shall be!
 Frien's of Pallas, curler fellows,
Winter swallows skimming free
   On loch and swamp savanna,
In their wanderings over earth,
Country's fame and Freedom's worth
Shall be theirs to blazon forth
   By manly Curliana."

O, Curliana! thine 's the glee
To mak' ane's life desired to be—
Active, social, healthy, spree,
   The type o' Caledonia!
Rheumatism, gout, or spleen,
 Asthma whaizem, cholic squeezem,
Ague freezem, all there 's nane
   Wi' those o' thy arcana!
Hog-score—to drug and medicine!
Come, wield the thundering channelstane,
And, sweating, souple soop him in,
   Chieftains o' Curliana!

We bliss our stars we are not lost
'Neath torrid suns to fry and roast,
But under zero skies of frost
   Can snuff cauld Caledonia—

Can here as brithers meet at home,
  Here as brithers meet wi' ithers
At our fathers' hoary game
      In great Americana !
The year is lovely in its bower
Of song, bud, fragrance, fruit, and flower,
But skipping on its crystal floor
      Is glorious Curliana !

———

...THE KYLE LASSIES AS OUR
... THE BURNS FESTIVAL 1876.

———

But now the lassies in their hand
Hae ta'en the thing to gar it stand;
Hence, as if by enchanter's wand,
    Scenes a' around
Bright, bright as those of fairy-land
    Transport—astound !

'T is said, in mony a dissertation,
That woman is the coronation—
The masterpiece of vast creation
    Set in the van,
In every age, stage, or relation,
    " Help-meet " to man.

Wha stops at first his squalling mouth;
Wha guides his tott'ring steps thro' youth;
Wha combs and sheds his ringlets smooth
    Pleased wi' the bother,
And trains him how to lisp the truth?
    A loving mother.

And neist to her he ca's his mither,
When cares and troubles round him gather,
Or sickness maks his strength to wither,
    Say wha can pity
And ha'd the head up like nae ither?
    Dear Meg, his titty.

Wha was it took an active say
In boyhood bargain, broil, and play,
And couthie, ranting night and day
      Redressed each want ?
Was it not she—sage, young, yet gray—
      Ycleped the aunt ?

And wha 's the ane that wi' her glamor
Sets beardless boys to learn love's grammar,
Ay ! bach'lor grubs to *amo* stammer
      Despite the penny,
And in his heart for aye embalm her ?
      'T is charming Jenny.

Say wad na hame be just a dungeon
Devoid o' comfort or communion,
All, all disorder, all disunion
      And family strife,
Without the prudent, mild dominion
      Of sonsie wife ?

And has not she our best respects
Wha oft ensconced us frae our licks—
Wha humorsome to her wee Jacks
      And Sandies many,
The muckle A's taught thro' her specks—
      Our douce auld grannie ?

And last not least we sing the maid
Of pious, charitable deed,
That like a Dorcas to our need
　　　　Hath nobly risen!
All hearty praise and thanks be paid
　　　　To Bess, our cousin!

JOCK'S LODGE.

READ AT THE LODGE ANNIVERSARY, SEPTEMBER 7, 1856.

My social friends, met on our birth-night,
Ye call for rhymes to aid our mirth right;
But not being gifted by the muse
Nae rhymes hae I, sae plead excuse.
If not admitted, she must romp now
In some nonsensical impromptu.

We hae among us different lodges,
Wi' words, and signs, and grips, and badges,
Some yclept Masons, and some Odd Fellows,
And some, (I like the name,) Good Fellows,
Wi' many ithers orthodox;
But this ane, designated Jock's—
Say, is it not a perfect hoax?

Hark ! and I'll tell you what this lodge is,
And strangers be yerselves the judges.
Its name is Scotch—its members clannish ;
Yet when ye set them down outlan'ish,
Mark that they have (and I will thank ye)
Made now their hame the land o' Yankee ;
Their future destiny 's inwove
With his, be 't weel or woe, by Jove !
Their happiest hours when thus they gather
To hail him as a frien' and brither
Wi' sangs o' Scotland, their respected mither.

Ane feature o' the lodge's mission
Is mind-improvement—self-tuition.
And that their sweethearts once a year
May wi' their blessed presence cheer,
Their bachelor meetings a' enhance,
This night 's devoted to the dance.
Then blow your loudest, honest piper !
And let the dousest loup a skipper !
For me, my boys, not shod wi' sandals,
I 'll shout hurra ! and snuff the candles.

Anither object o' the club
Is native countrymen to dub
Americans soon as they land
On famed Cuyahoga's bluffy strand ;

Make Cleveland's halls of hospitality
Show Scottish clans' conviviality,
And cause re-echo Erie's shore
With their sweet minstrelsy of yore,
When social love fans patriotic,
The joy, the bliss, O how ecstatic!

    About their secrets, grips, and word,
The lassies ken them a', I 've heard—
Learn of them then their *amo* grammar;
Yet mind! beware o' Jenny's glamor!
For me—but I am sae new fangle—
The Yankee gals do most entangle;
And as I see a number present
Whose beaux are Scotch, behaving decent,
In these my notions I 'm not single.
Wal!—an't it right that we should mingle;
But—thank your patience—I must end my jingle.

A WELCOME.

———

AT THE BANQUET GIVEN BY THE BURNS CURLING CLUB OF
CLEVELAND TO THE CALEDONIAN CLUB OF BUFFALO,
JANUARY 15, 1868.

——— ,

Good fellow-curlers! to our city
Wi' open heart and han' we greet ye,
And at this social board wad treat ye
      As brithers leel;
   Wi' Highland welcome, sirs, we meet ye
      To play the Spiel!

And so you beat us—very near—
What then? have at ye, boys, next year;
For tho' the sport we hold sae dear
      Depends on skill,
A slippery game of chance-like share
      Is mony a Spiel.

Nae matter how the medal 's gone—
A besom-toss when a' is done!
The object aimed at is the fun
        Of friendship's deal—
Renewed or new acquaintance won
        At national Spiel!

Then let true sentiment go round,
Let merry toast and song abound,
Let humor broad and wit profound
        Rouse laughter's peal,
Till Yankee palaces resound
        Auld Scotia's Spiel!

Rise in thy piper majesty!
O Anderson! and let us hae,
To suit this gathering o' the free,
        Some piobrach'd shrill!
Come, blaw your very best o' glee,
        And charm our Spiel!

Still in our minds we fondly cherish
The pitted match of neighbor parish,
When at some shot decisive for us,
        In curler zeal
The besom round our head we 'd flourish,
        And boast the Spiel!

" Last of my fields* " was on the Nith,
Where I did soop wi' a' my pith ;
The wives against the lassies, beth
      For load o' meal
To mak' some auld and puir anes blyth,
      Had matched the Spiel !

But while as clansmen o' the heather
Thus happy met wi' ane anither,
Our loving Jonathan and brither
      We also hail !
"At hame ! sit forrit !"—let 's together
      Enjoy the Spiel !

Our countries beth the first on earth !
The same in language, laws, and birth,
Now lately wed by cable girth,
      Shall ever feel
The kindred glow, as round their hearth
      They end the Spiel !

Detested be that traitor loon,
And cursed by all the powers aboon,
That wad destroy, like auld Mahoun,
      Our country's weal !
His be the lake where ice there 's none,
      Nor jovial Spiel !

---

* A phrase of Ossian.

Gie gambler fops their oyster trash,
Their pies and puddings and sic hash;
But if ye 'd please a curler's wish
        Gie beef and greens,
Time immemorial the dish
        Of channelstanes.

Lang may ye, wi' your worthy head,
Of every club still keep the lead,
(Wi' ane exception, this is said
        Between oursel',)
Your courtesy and curler deed
        Deserve each Spiel!

CURLING SONG.

Tune: "Bonnie Dundee."

Come on, my brave curlers! in life's slippery game
We a' hae a part, and should a' hae an aim;
The rules are before us, and let us rejoice
We may one and all gain an Infinite prize.

In choosing the course of life's rink let there be
Nae prejudice warpings to set us a-gee,
And when passion is keen, or alluring the ice,
With caution let 's guard a' temptation to vice.

And lest ours be shame and the skip become wroth
Let none o' us lag on the hog-score o' sloth;
When drug is the play, and we canna' get up,
With the broom perseverance, boys, swoop! let us swoop!

To reach our ambition—to rest on the tee,
Let 's down thro' the crowd jostle in honestly ;
Beth in-wick and out-wick, strike, guard, chap, and lie,
"Fair play, love, and friendship," each clan's slogan cry.

'Gainst every opponent of evil to cope,
Place firmly your foot on the crampit of hope,
And nerved wi' resolve play wi' science and skill,
Resigning to fortune the rest, good or ill.

Should the play o' our neighbor be not just the thing
Let 's chip him obligingly into the ring ;
Let all of our stanes by some virtue be named,
And our actions and words by the Graces proclaimed.

When done is our playing, when ended life's game,
'Neath the shades o' the evening we 'll then toddle hame :
O, boys ! may it be to a Supper Above,
Prepared a reward of true merit and love.

CURLER'S SONG.

TUNE: " BERKS OF ABERFALDY."

While gamblers stake on cards and dice
Wealth, honor, and domestic peace,
A manly game upon the ice
   Be ours on old Cuyahoga.

CHORUS.

Fellow-curlers, let us go, let us go, let us go ;
Fellow-curlers, let us go to the ice on auld Cuyahoga.

To gie the cheek health's rosy smile,
To brace the nerve for coming toil,
To banish care, let 's out awhile
   To the ice on auld Cuyahoga.
CHORUS—Fellow-curlers, let us go, etc.

Wha would be sic a cauldrif chiel
As at the ingle cringe for beil
While gloriously goes on the speil
   On the ice o' auld Cuyahoga.

CHORUS—Fellow-curlers, let us go, etc.

The dewy lawn besprent wi' flowers,
Or feathered choir in fragrant bowers,
Lack half the charms o' winter's stores
   On the ice on auld Cuyahoga.

CHORUS—Fellow-curlers, let us go, etc.

Though far frae Scotland's lochs and hame,
Yet our forefathers' favorite game
Shall we pursue, and a' its fame
   Be ours on auld Cuyahoga.

CHORUS.

Fellow-curlers, let us go, let us go, let us go ;
Fellow-curlers, let us go to the flats on auld Cuyahoga.

THE PICNIC..

HELD AT ROCKY RIVER, 1869.

Brother knights of the Thistle, viscounts, dukes, and lairds!
Eh!—'Merican kings of proud shanties and yards!
Dame Nature to woo in her sweet solitudes
And hold a Scotch picnic, we 've ta'en to the woods.
As a park, Rocky River we 've often heard broached,
And now we will see if it 's Scottish or scotched.
Let 's then wi' our Jockies and Jennies survey
Frae yon height the wide landscape and scenes o' the day.
O what a rare prospect spreads round and around;
Northward Lake Erie sets limitless bound
Far, far as the eye spans the concave expanse;
The white sails of commerce recede and advance,
While steamers puff music and lead on the dance;
The fisherman's boats and the pleasure yachts grand
Like motes in the sunbeam float nearer the strand.
See! frolicsome boys from the niche on the steep
In glory primeval leap into the deep;

14

Like so many Leanders, stout, worthy, and brave,
They buffeting sport with the amorous wave.
Say Scotland, is not our Lake Erie sae fair
To thy own classic Katrine all worthy compare!
If eastward and southward we turn our rapt gaze,
The picture how charming, despite the thick haze.
Above the tall forest, a hundred of steeples
Point upward and glittering preach to the peoples.
Where huge manufactory-turrets arise
Dense volumes of smoke dress in mourning the skies.
Hark! hark ye! 't is industry's buzz that we hear;
The hammer of artizan falls on our ear—
Albeit in thy suburbs now little is seen
Of thy beauty, O Cleveland! for Summer's rich green,
The proud Forest City 's miscalled not I ween.
But why wide thus ramble—at hand and in view
The callants (now bearded) youth's pastimes renew.
Pleased echo repeats thro' the still woody mazes
Auld Scotia's braid accent and weel-kenned hame phrases.
See! yonder 's a party from fourteen to twenty,
Striped tartan and bonnet to flourish the shinty;
Here to the soft strains of the pibroch are seen
Young lads wi' their lassies tip-toe on the green;
There some more athletic go hop, stride, and jump,
Or, supple, the summersault turn off the stump.
The boys Rob and Tam, slipped away frae the rest,
Are after blae berries or little bird-nest;
Not fond of sic visits the rabbit and squirrel
Disdainful turn at them their tails in a swirl.

Whist! voice of the cuckoo or thrush did ye think?
'T is the yell o' the cat-bird or strange bobolink.
Ho! peace-time at past-time—now 'neath maple bowers,
On Nature's own carpet enameled with flowers,
In family groups all are squatted to pree
The baskets of guid wife, while the lassie sae free
Without etiquette passes bannock and cheese
Wi' ither fine dainties the palate to please;
While fresh frae the spring on the brow o' the hill
Man, mither, and bairn take their wallawaugh fill.
But bodily refreshment sufficeth us not—
The feast o' the soul is what pleases a Scot;
Hence joke, sang, and sentiment freely go round
Till the listening woodlands with cheerings resound.

    *   *   *   *   *   *   *   *

Now here 's to Laird Tisdale and a' o' that ilk,
    For kind Highland welcome extended this day;
That he aye may have plenty of porritch and milk
    Caledonians grateful ever shall pray.

SCOTCHMEN, RALLY!

AIR: "STAR-SPANGLED BANNER."

Who, who is for freedom, the Union, and right?
　Wake, clans of the North! loud the tocsin is sounding
And beacons are blazing on ilka green height!
　The proud Southern loons on their war steeds are bounding,
Are spoiling our forts, are blockading our ports,
Are marching to beard us in home-sweet resorts!
Up, Scotchmen! none laggard! like sons of the brave!
Say the Star-Spangled Banner in glory shall wave!

To ask now the cause of the present campaign
　We halt not: enough kens a Scotchman about it
When tauld that its origin 's slavery's chain
　And tyrant usurpation the end if not routed.
For freedom and law then our claymores we 'll draw
And, God on our side, in the right we 'll hurra!
Will help to unfetter our country's last slave
That her Star-Spangled Banner more glorious may wave!

Shall Reuben-divisions cause searching of hearts?
   Or Meroz-neutrality curses most weighty?
Shall Ashur-like, Scotchmen abide in their marts,
   And not to the help of the Lord with the mighty?*
Forbid it, by all that we sacred do call!
By mothers, wives, sisters, and children small!
An on-looking world marks how we behave:
Caledonians! the Star-Spangled banner shall wave!

---

* Judges, v.

"SCOTS WHA HAE."

———

Scots wha hae come here to bide!
Scots whase sires for freedom died!
Up! and in your country's pride
      Strike for Libertie!

Now the South rebellious rears!
See! its servile army dares!
Hark! the traitor Davis swears,
      " Long live Slaverie!"

Wha can neutral stand a fool?
Wha submit to sic misrule?
Wha wink at or be the tool
      Of base Tyrannie?

Wha 's for Union, order, law?
Wha 's for freedom gi'en to a'?
Let him glorious stand or fa',
      Ranked with braverie!

By Fort Sumter, by our slain,
By oppression's cruel chain,
We shall frae our flag the stain
    Wipe eternallie!

Lay the proud enslavers low!
Rebels fall in every foe!
Heaven and justice nerve the blow!
    On to victorie!

WALLACE.

ADDRESS TO SCOTCH AMERICANS, FOR AID TO COMPLETE THE
NATIONAL WALLACE MONUMENT, SCOTLAND.

Scots wha hae of Wallace read !
Scots by birth or Yankee bred,
Welcome shall be now your aid
     To his memory !

Now unfinished to this hour
Stands his monumental tower :
In your patriotic power
     On to victory !

Wha that boasts Auld Scotia's name,
Glorying in her heroes' fame,
Yet responds not to this claim,
     Let him traitor be !

When proud feudal times are gone—
England, Scotland merged in one—
Save this deed historic none
      Reads of enmity.

For the independence won
By our dauntless fathers gone
We will help to raise a stone,
      Sons of liberty!

Countrymen at home, rejoice!
Yankee-Scots of enterprise
Lay the cope-stone in the skies,
      Grateful that they 're free.

THE SNUFF-BOX.

———

PRESENTED TO WILLIAM LOWRIE, PRESIDENT OF THE
ST. ANDREW'S SOCIETY.

———

Sir, hearing that you 've struck on ile,
And 's gaun to live on 'Troleum soil,
Your countrymen and frien's, meanwhile
      The freedom take
To gie ye something in the style
      Of marked respect.

As a St. Andrew's son you 've been
A charitable chiel, I ween;
And as a curler-fellow keen
      You 've played your part;
To lose ye, man, we rub our een,
      Sad at the heart.

To aid a brither in distress,
To help a Yankee boy to guess,
To gie the festive hall its grace
      And dance attraction,
Your purse, your noddle, and your phiz
      Were aye in action.

Esteemed amang us was your merit ;
But chiefly 'cause you did inherit
Of sense and fun a kindred spirit
      This 'bacco box
To you 's presented ; take and wear it
      For us, your folks.

Lang may ye live to tap its lid
And frae it thumb the peacefu' quid ;
Altho' it holds a stinking weed,
      Yet you can make it
In social circle speak the deed
      Of worth respectit.

RESPONSE.

———

To the Toast, "Our Sister Societies in America," at the
Manx Society Festival.

———

Mr. President—

    Yours humbly and truly would here represent,
In the name of Auld Scotia's patron saint,
A sister society known by his name,
Benevolence chiefly its pride and its aim.
    And first let us thank you for bidding us here
To partake of your friendship in festival cheer.
With hearty good will and in rivalry none,
Except in the deeds of benevolence shown,
We wish you Gude-speed—all success to your cause
And to each anniversary crowning applause.
    If laws the same governed our dear natal hames
And made us one people in customs and aims,
In this our adopted why should there not be
Reciprocal friendship to fan charity?

Nor doubt I that this, sir, will meet the consent
Of your three-legged, lang-legged, bare-legged saint,
Who seems to be one rather fond of a sling
And determined to dance us the Highlandman fling;
Giving Albion and Scotia and Erin a kick
To spur them or spurn them all down to auld Nick.
As for our St. Andrew he looks not so jolly;
He, on his cross leaning, appears melancholy
And seems to say, "Callants, beware of all folly
And be under St. Jonathan loyal and holy,"
A piece of advice that if followed might be
Of service to us, as you all will agree.

To emigrants landing, Americans seem
A proud, haughty people, above their esteem;
But with better acquaintance such views are removed,
And manners once censured are chosen and loved.
Yes, Jonathan 's prudent, suspicious, 'cute,
And rightly of foreigners keeps a look-out
Till they 're with his interests identified—then
They find him the noblest and kindest of men.
We speak from experience—friends, what say you?
I know you 'll respond that the sentiment 's true.

*   *   *   *   *   *   *   *

The lands that we left, as the spots of our birth,
The scenes of our boyhood and juvenile mirth—
Dear, dear to us ever, remembered shall be
At festive rejoicings afar o'er the sea.

Yet the land that we live in, the home of our choice,
Claims more our esteem by our hopes and our joys.
In yonder kirkyard honored forefathers sleep,
But here our loved bairnies laugh 'round us or weep.
America! with thee our destiny 's cast;
O what to the present and future 's the past?
Thy grand institutions—our children's—we honor
And exult 'neath the folds of thy star-spangled banner.
    Then fill up a bumper—with cheers three times three,
The toast, "Young America, glorious and free!"

"QUOCUNQUE JECERIS STABIT.'

READ AT THE FESTIVAL OF THE MONA RELIEF SOCIETY.

On the shores of the lovely Lake Erie we roam,
   Afar from our sweet native strand;
Yet yearly we 'll meet and thus sing as at home—
   " Throw me which way you will, sir, I stand !"

Be it so that the English, Scotch, Irish, and Dutch
   In the name of their saints rally grand—
They 're myths all, while ours—the good Wilson 's not such—
   " Turn him what way you will, sir, he 'll stand."

From time immemorial queen of the seas
   Sat Mona, with trident in hand,
Till Sandy the Second of Scotland did seize—
   " But tho' every way thrown she did stand."

The Neds and the Harrys of England likewise
   Did wrest from our sires their land ;
Yet still—(and what better are they of the prize)—
   " Thrown which way you will, sir, we stand."

To joy there 's a dance, and to care there 's a kick,
   To tyranny rowels to brand.
With the world we are racing—a match for Old Nick :
   " Throw which way you will, sir, we stand."

For no misdemeanor, dear isle, wast thou left—
   Thy bounds would not let us expand—
A home for our children was sought by the shift—
   " Throw us which way you will, sir, we stand."

At home, independence and peace was our lot
   And here, too, we 'll fortune command ;
We 've left not behind us the schooling we got—
   " Throw us which way you will, sir, we stand."

And should a loved countryman wander in need,
   A dollar is his on demand,
That he among strangers may hold up his head—
   " Throw which way you will we still stand !"

TOASTS AND SENTIMENTS AT SCOTTISH
FESTIVALS.

———

SCOTLAND.

Her heathery hills and primrose glens,
Her flowery meads and oaten plains,
Her frowning cliffs and warlike cairns,
Her gowany braes and purling burns,
Her artizans and sons of genius,
Her bonny lassies, each a Venus—
These one and all let us remember
When thus we meet last o' November.

THE HAGGIS.

All hail, thou crowning dish of a' the feast !
Which to a Scotchman hath a special zest.
At sight o' thee associations fine
Wake up the soul and speak of " auld lang syne,"
Bring heather hill, the gowan glowing green,
And haunted burnie a' before our een ;
Give back ance mair the laughter to the ear
Of weddin, kirn, or new year's social cheer.

15

AMERICA.

What land, America, like thee
For genius and true liberty,
For mountain, lake, and forest tree
    And mighty classic river ?

What land, save Caledonia,
With these characteristics a' ?
And what is better—we can ca'
    Both countries ours forever !

THE SCOTCH COTTAGER'S FIRESIDE.

An ingle blazing bonnilee ; a sweepit clean hearth-stane ;
The chairs arranged in order ; the dresser decked in sheen ;
Auld baudrins thrumming on the hud ; the kitten bent on
    play ;
The collie splenart in the nook ; the cricket chirping gay ;
Young Jenny for her dozen cut birrs busy at the wheel,
And Aunty Meg, wi' measured click, turns round and round
    the reel ;
The mither in the cradle rocks a rather wakrife bairn ;
While on a book the guid man reads that a' may something
    learn.

THE SCHOOL HOUSE.

At yon brae-foot where trips the wimpling burn
    Sedate arose the well frequented school
Where we attendant first to read did learn.

Do we imagine merely like the fool,
  Or do we really see the long notched stool,
The desk, the books, the copies, and the taas
  Which smick-smack o'er the fingers caused the yowl?
For ill said questions, or school-broken laws,
Oft to our shame we felt right smartly what it was.

Now peace-time, past-time comes! out! out! hurra!
  See! each pursues his favorite game of fun,
Some wield the shintie, kicks or clods the ba';
  Others athletic wrestle, leap, and run;
  By yonder squad the cats are lost and won;
By this the bowls are played wi' gabbling sounds;
  And in that circle sweet the pierie 's spun;
While wide excursive o'er the adjacent grounds
Ane skuds a fancied hare, pursued by yelping hounds.

SCOTLAND AND AMERICA—THE LAND WE LEFT AND THE LAND WE LIVE IN.

    Oaten cakes and Yankee lakes
      Beat creation fairly,
    As place o' birth and scenes o' worth
      Till death we 'll prize them dearly.

OUR SISTER SOCIETIES.

Co-laborers in charity upon the social plan,
May there be no disparity of sentiment but one,
The vieing with each other in doing what we can
To aid a needfu' brither—a friendless countryman.

THE PRESS.

Of public weal the guard,
Of truth the flag unfurled,
Of liberty the sword,
And light of the whole world.

THE BONNIE LASSIES.

Up! three hearty cheers!
For the sweet, lovely dears,
  Man's solace, perfecter, and joy!
Of all gems the best,
And when put to the test
  The gold without any alloy!
Without them what would we do?
Without them what could we do?
  Say, married man, bachelor, boy?

THE HEROES AND PATRIOTS OF SCOTLAND AND AMERICA.

Gallants, wha by their actions one's led to suppose
Had an excellent relish for mush and kail brose;
Love of country apparent, their destiny's star,
Presiding in peace and directing in war.

A HANDFUL OF VERSES.

ON VISITING THE PLACE OF MY BIRTH AND THE HOME OF MY YOUTH.

O Courance ! dearest spot on earth, to me
  The fairest, loveliest, wheresoe'er I go.
Oft have I hailed with childhood ecstasy
  Thy woodbine-muffled cottage—now not so,
  But with the silent tear of heartfelt woe.
No more its fragrant bowers of evergreen
  My father, mother, or dear brethren know ;
No more they round its pleasant hearth convene—
A stranger family 's there, and walks the sylvan scene.

Gane is the biggin' now which gave me birth ;
  Its site now fragrant with the clover white ;
Here it was mine first to behold green earth
  And welkin blue in all its gems bedight ;
  Here learned to ca' things by their names aright.
As Summer's herald, jocund and alone,
  (The oldest thing in memory still bright,)
Perched on yon thorn sang " cuckoo !" I anon
" Cuckoo !" replied with imitative tone.

Oft hae I guddled in that burnie clear
　For speckled trout, and naething catched at night.
As often hae I dug in sod-dyke here
　　The bumm-bee-bink wi' spirits gay and light;
　　Or wi' the wasp hae held a desperate fight,
Spruce twig my sword and shield, till in the lug
　　Wi' venomed dirk stabbed, I was put to flight:
To avenge the deed, at dark they got when snug
A cataract boiling hot, poured forth frae ponderous jug.

Many 's the times on these green knolls I 've lain
　And eyed the laverock, like a little bead,
Soaring in ether high and warbling fine—
　　Ah! gaudy flutterer, dost thou in pride
　　Before me pass my state now to deride?
Well I remember, when nor rhymes my head
　　Nor cares my mind perplexed, with lightsome stride
Chasing the butterfly thro' that green mead,
As it from flower to floweret wary from me fled.

Sing on sweet thrush! and thou gay blackbird sing!
　For kindness past have I not now your song?
Was 't you I fed ere ye had note or wing;
　　Or are ye, say, their offspring—great-grand-young?
　　If such you be attend: "These shrubs among
My childhood strollings found your forbears' nest.
　　Bare gorbs they were; we bade them dread no wrong,
But curious oft their gapings wide redressed,
And to our cheek fond pressed their half-fledged panting
　　　breast."

*   *   *   *   *   *   *   *   *

These were the days—days when nor clouds of care
   Nor mists of sorrow dimmed youth's azure skies.
All, all was blossom, song, and sunshine clear !
   But now they 're fled with all their charming joys,
   On me no more fair flushing to arise.
O precious youth ! I never prized thy worth
   Till years of moil too late did make me wise :
Had I but better spent these hours of mirth
I ablins might have bettered that my humble birth !

As when fell hawk dread hovering o'er sweet glade
   Darts down upon, and bears aloft his prey—
Some little tenants of the covert shade
   Which harmless reared their young the livelong day :
   The hapless young bereaved of their stay
Take to the woodlands, chirping void of cheer,
   So death, invidious, snatched to heaven away
The best of parents from their children here,
Who weep their loss dispersed thro' this world wide and drear.

Yes, we have lost the guardians of our youth
   Who made our welfare their delight and care ;
Who taught us virtue, piety, and truth
   By precept sage and by example rare.
   For were they not—but what by grace they were—
To man how honest, and to God how true !
   Now modesty forbids us to declare.
This we may say, "Like us a very few
Were by Heaven blessed with such parents two."

As children of such parents let us then
   Live, walking blameless in their pious ways,
That so we may like them without a stain
    Pass thro' this world and end in peace our days,
    Cheered with the hope that we with them shall raise
Songs of salvation to the One in Three,
    Voices and hearts attuned to holiest praise,
Forming a part of heaven's great family
Still dearer to each other—Oh, when shall this be!

Most honored parents, now the blessed dead!
   Unto the memory ever, ever dear!
Do ye behold, or know you what betide
    Your children in their lonely wanderings here?
    Bear ye not yet for them parental care?
Unseen and gentle as the summer gale
    Commissioned gracious do you hover near
And ministrant them prompt how to prevail
When trials mark them, or when spiritual foes assail?

Why then, as lost to us, for you bewail,
   When now perhaps ye do us more real good
Than when encumbered with your bodies frail?
    Can we suppose a mother's feelings could
    Die with her and be buried in a shroud?
Or that the enjoyments of the blessed above
    Will supersede her great solicitude?
Hark! hark! is that her well known voice of love
Whispering condolence in that wont frequented grove?

What tho' to many your remembrance dies,
   What tho' no stone your humble worth may tell,
Yet in your children's bosoms sacred rise
   For you proud monuments—there fresh ye dwell,
   And shall—until their own departure-knell !
Oft in their wanderings thither they 'll repair
   To view these fields and taste that crystal well
Which long supplied you with sufficient fare,
And filial, fondly cherish your remembrance dear.

TO A GOLD PEN AND PENCIL-CASE.

PRESENTED TO THE AUTHOR BY THE CALEDONIAN LITERARY
SOCIETY.

———

Thou pen! presented sly and witty
By Caledonian literati,
With caligraphic flourish pritty
    Come, thank the donor.
Fail thou in this, the mair 's the pity
    And my dishonor.

Thou 'rt here a tribute of esteem,
Wi' story flattering in their name;
Now tho' we 're made by sic a gem
    Beth proud and braw,
Yet we must own that we 've nae claim
    For such ava.

Say then that I by grace inherit,
And that I do discard all merit—
Greatly delinquent, tho' in spirit
    Indeed quite willing,
And beg their patience not to jeer at
      Our mony a failing.

They ca' me "faither," but a faither
We ne'er had been without a mither—
Themselves all jointly put together—
    Sae at the best
We 're only but a self-taught brither
      Amang the rest.

Have we some little favors shown ?
Have we some puny efforts done ?
The motive chief for such when known
    Will speak of self :
Dearer to me this social fun
      Than paltry pelf.

*   *   *   *   *   *   *

Sae thank them kindly, thank them weel ;
Remember thou 'rt nae stumpy quill ;
And tell them how I gratful feel
    For sic a favor ;
Yes, that thy service and mysel'
      Are their's forever !

When death my fingers freezes cold,
And I nae longer thee can hold,
I deed thee—sacred friendship's gold,
    Precious and rare—
To ane wha keeps thee, bought nor sold,
    A relic dear!

INAUGURATION OF COMMODORE PERRY'S STATUE.

CLEVELAND, SEPTEMBER 10, 1860.

"We 've met the en'my—they 're ours!"
We heard thee in our darkest hours,
And now, when war no longer lowers
    O, gallant Perry!
We crown thee with triumphal flowers
    Hero of Erie!

Ye mystic brethren, raise his shrine
By square and bevel, plumb and line,
Let art and genius all combine
    That gallant Perry
May stand revealed in bold design
    Hero of Erie.

Let military corps parade ;
Let naval battle be displayed ;
Let citizens of every grade
      This day be cheerie,
That all due honors may be paid
      To him of Erie !

Peace to the dead of Put-in-Bay !
And in the front ranks of the day
Set the survivors of the fray
      Not lame nor weary :
Long may the laurel crown their gray,
      Heroes of Erie !

Who was the enemy met in war ?
The victor chiefs of Trafalgar.
Where England gave to France a scar
      She long did carry,
But England grasped no stripe or star
      On our Lake Erie.

She thought, as " Mistress of the seas "
To impress or do what she might please ;
" Free trade and sailor-right-degrees "
      Became the query,
Which was resolved in gallant ease
      On glorious Erie !

To keep in memory his renown ;
To tell his deeds need not a stone ;
In hearts American they 're shown,
      And cherished dear, aye :
By this is grateful homage done
      To the brave of Erie.

Rhode Island proud may boast his birth,
But the achievements of his worth
Are for the South as well as North—
      Yes, better, hear ye !
Are blessings prized o'er all the earth.
      Hail ! chief of Erie !

So long as Freedom spurns her foes,
Or heart with love of country glows,
Or thundering o'er Niagara flows
      The flood of Erie,
In sculpture, painting, verse, and prose
      Shall live our Perry !

MAUTHE DHU, OR BLACK DOG.

A MANX LEGEND.

> " Of shapes that walk
> At dead of night, and clank their chains, and wave
> The torch of hell around the murderer's bed."
> —*Akenside.*

In days of yore when fairies rife
Scared honest folk out of their life,
Peel Castle, Man, was then the haunt
Of Mauthe Dhu, a goblin gaunt.
Jet black and curly was its hair,
And then its een—how they did glare !
'T was never heard to bark or growl,
But in its face—ah, what a scowl !
Something abhorrent in each feature
Bespoke it an unearthly creature !

Say, native Manx man, ye yoursel'
Hae seen the castle, and can tell

Its massy wall—and a' about it—
Auld grannie's story never doubted.
Say how this fort, when in its glory,
Had flight of stairs to upper story;
On ilka side was mony a room
Wi' winnock sma' to shed a gloom:
How in this ane was stowed provision,
And in that ither ammunition;
How on the roof was watchman's berth,
To spy the pirate on the firth;
And of the chamber where the soldiers
When not on duty were the lodgers;
And of its passage underground,
Which thro' the chapel led profound
To where the captain with his wife
In quiet spent a warfare life.

Well, on a night of bleak December
The guard all met in this their chamber
In circle round the blazing hearth
Tried to allay with songs of mirth
The irksome bodings in their breast,
For Mauthe Dhu, unwelcome guest,
(Not splennart on the floor asleep
Like hound chase-weary) watch did keep,
With een most stern, and ope-mouth foaming,
None dare to do aught unbecoming.

About this sprite was something strange,
Tho' the whole castle was its range,
Yet this guard-room seemed to have been
Its favored haunt—here mostly seen.
From out the subterranean walk
At candle-light 't was seen to stalk,
And take its stand before the fire.
Till rising day made it retire.
Hence, when the keys at curfew knell
Were carried to the captain's cell,
Twa went, by turns, to save affright,
(This was the custom every night,)
To face the ghost, some twa might dare it,
But one alone—O, Pluto, spare it!
There was enlisted in this guard
One born at sea, of life unstarred,
A sceptic, heaven-daring fellow,
With smuggled rations ever mellow!
That swore by devil, hell, and conscience,
"Fairies and worrie-cows are nonsense;
That Trinon's monster big Buggane,
That Rushen's dame of nigger tan,
That Mauthe Dhu, the present terror,
Are bugbears all and gossip error;
And such I prove!"   This said, the keys
(Despite of all remonstrances)
He took, and flourishing did rush
Into the pass—and all was hush!

When miners touch with fuse the train
And breathless wait the exploding scene,
So stood the guard and eyed the vault,
Wondering what would be the result.
Mauthe, too, gone! None dared to follow!
Hark! what a fiendish scream and hallo!
The man must ha' been charmed by witches
And now he's in the devil's clutches!
Yes, be it Satan, dog, or bogle,
Desperate must be the unseen struggle!

* * * * * *
Our hero comes, but, by the powers,
Sobered and creeping on all fours!
Spirited away, what folks did see
Was of him just the effigy!
Vacant his stare, his visage grim;
Dumb—not a word was got from him.
On the third day his limbs did rest—
No requiem sung by friend or priest.
To save another like mischanter,
The pious folk of Peel instanter
Blocked up the passage at both ends,
So Mauthe Dhu nae mair attends.
The whys and wherefores of its history
Till lately slept an awful mystery.
A Yankee to the task found equal
Unravels all and tells the sequel.

Of parents Manx was Rabbin born;
Of mind, an antiquarian turn;
In childhood oft he 'd heard this tale
Frae mither lips, agape and pale;
When grown to man he took a sail
To see his father's native isle—
Inspect Peel Castle and *incog.*
Learn more about the Mauthe Dhug.
Weel—mark him now stripped to the sark,
With mattock and with lanthron dark.
Opening the passage up anew
And rummaging it through and through.
To his agreeable surprise
In secret niche he haply spies
An earthen pot, three gallon size,
Crammed full of gold and silver treasure—
(To-day he counts it at his leisure)—
Over it was a vellum cover
With old black letter scribbled over,
Nae doubt a sprite communication,
And this its literal translation:
"And must I write my last confession?
Oh, that it would procure remission!
Where the Neb river greets the tide,
In fisher's cottage now decayed
Annie, the young and guileless, lived,
Of parents lately both bereaved.

I woo'd and won her trust and heart
By acting the dissembler's part.
That treasure, by her father left her,
Was all that I, poor wretch, was after.
One night the chance seemed so provoking,
Blessed with her kiss and harmless joking,
No witness present but thyself—
O, cursed appetite for pelf!
With protestation high and solemn,
And pointing to the Holy Volume
Her eye a moment to divert—
I plunged the knife into her heart,
Throbbing with love! a meaning glare
You got! I, a portentous stare!
As gasping she her last did breathe.
Since then you 've dogged my every path,
And horrified my guilty conscience,
Despite my atheistic nonsense.
Here that same night the pot I hid,
Yet oft since then to lift the lid
In vain hae tried—thou ever there
In all thy terrible—to dare.
I could no longer—crazed wi' drinking,
Unfit for life, for death, for thinking,
With spurning kick and oath profane
I spoke you!—mercy!—ah!—what then?
Your mission finished—not my pain!"

Now ye wha read this fearful tale
To mark the moral dinna fail:
Red secret crime is hard to smother;
Murder will out some time or other:
Haunted by goblin, de'il, or ghost,
A guilty conscience daunts the most.

TO THE PRAISE OF TEA, AS USED BY THE PEASANTRY OF SCOTLAND.

———

Come a' ye wives wha grace your ingle
Wi' tea-pot, kettle, or wi pingle,
And join me in my hamely jingle,
      While I essay
A theme, 't will " mak' your ears to tingle,"
      A cup o' Tea!

Aye! let love-smitten bard the lassies
Extol above angelic classes,
And drunken poets o'er their glasses
      Sing whiskey gay;
We mount another gait Parnasses
      In cup o' Tea.

When man first hails the worl' loud greeting
Prophetic o' the ills awaiting,
Auld wives and houdies ha'd a meeting,
   And gossips say,
Wow! but they get a hearty treating
   To cup o' Tea.

When man is made a christen'd critter,
(A deed the sooner done the better,)
It wad be but a bummeled matter
   On holiday,
Did it conclude not wi' a clatter
   O'er cup o' Tea.

When crouse-fond couple plan a wedding,
In lordly ha' or cottage haudin',
Their execution o't a bad ane
   Without the—the—
I dinna mean to say the beddin'—
   But cup o' Tea.

And when we 've to attend the bier
Of frien' or relative, most dear,
There 's naething has the balm to cheer,
   Or grief allay,
Like dropping th' affectionate tear
   In cup o' Tea.

On Sunday ere the kirk-bells tome,
When cotters' hired bairns come home
To get clean sark, or head a comb—
  A blessing they
Parental get, in grace's humm,
    'Fore cup o' Tea.

On New Year's day the porrach-goan
Lies whammled, and instead upon
The table guid wife's peastry 's shown
    'Bove fashion's sway,
A feast—the happiest! then is known
    O'er cup o' Tea.

At public festival occasion,
Or on eventful celebration,
The genius—taste o' every nation
    Is suited aye,
To mingle Attic conversation
    O'er cup o' Tea.

When bairns wi' sair wames yowl and gant;
When auld wives' heads are like to rent;
When love-lorn maids are 'bout to faint
    In fits away,
Administer the healing plant
    In cup o' Tea.

Begone ! ye deevil-ridden hags,
That to get lin'd your greedy bags,
Read cups to fools o' credulous lugs
       And fortunes spae !
Mixed ne'er shall be wi' your d——d drugs
       My cup o' Tea.

When for a fast I wad prepare ;
When hungry, tired, vexed wi' care ;
Or when I'm laid beth lank and spare
       . Disease's prey,
Just gie me life's elixir rare—
       A cup o' Tea.

And when at last we pant for breath,
And bid farewell to a' beneath,
To blunt the barbed dart o' death,
       While doctors pray,
As extreme unction, gi'e in faith
       A cup o' Tea.

Great cordial ! sure thou stand'st confessed,
The glorious substitute and best,
In place of our dram-drinking pest !
       Come crown my lay !
As choice of true teetotaler taste—
       Prime cup o' Tea.

'T is hell-forged alcoholian knife
That cuts the bond of peace, and strife
Creates 'twixt friends—'twixt man and wife !
   But rack-stick play
On all the ties o' social life
   'S a cup o' Tea.

In temp'rance name, then, my advice is,
Let all for tea-cups 'change their glasses ;
Nor longer like to cadger's asses
   In dram-shop bray,
When such pure, real, domestic bliss is
   In cup o' Tea.

TOBACCO.

———

I sing of Tobacco! Come help me chant,
Ye smokers and chewers, your wonderful plant;
Its use universal, its charms to enthral,
Its stench and its filth, yes, its poison and all.

Red man of the forest! of whose hunting ground
Our plant is a native, say, how was it found?
Aware of its virtues, O, when did your sires
Smoke the first pipe of peace or of war 'round their fires?

Three centuries, with most of their customs, have fled
Since Europe her whiskey exchanged for a quid;
But these two—the most damning of all—yet remain!
What figures can add up the victims they 've slain!

There 's aconite, alcohol, opium, bang,
Narcotical all and of serpentine fang!
But the most circumventive, most fatal, most fell,
Is nicotine, 'stilled from this smoke-soot of hell!

Tell us not of its use—its medicinal worth—
Its powers to inspire health, genius, and mirth!
'T is all a delusion, as baneful as vain,
That clenches more firmly our vile custom's chain!

Behold ye that smoker of pipe or cigar!
A monkey less antic you look at by far.
Like bellows his wrinkled jaws whiff out the funk—
Detestable more than the scent of a skunk.

Behold ye that chewer!—a wild billy-goat;
He ruminates ever and slavers about.
His breath is pollution itself, while his beard
With the juice of his fine cut is clammy besmeared.

Behold ye that snuffer! 't is farcical sport
To witness him take up his dust with a snort;
Then snotter and snob like an old glandered horse,
Till his sight becomes dim and his voice nasal hoarse!

And mark ye that pauper! In all of its forms
He riots a reptile, bewitched by its charms
An object of charity—censure, you mean—
Let him save his plug-pence and go wash and be clean!

Who knows not its evil effects and its filth?
The blaster of morals! the sapper of health!
Wherever corruption and crime do abound,
Tobacco, to stupefy, mummify, 's found!

Would were it confined to the low haunts of vice!—
In circles domestic it finds a proud place.
In God's house it even dares spit profanation—
Worse, worse than the "spoken of abomination!"

Young men! the cigar as the pestilence shun!
The first step to vice, it has thousands undone!
And O, ye gray-haired who are steeped in the guilt,
Come out of your filth and renewed men exult!

O for a Queen Bess! a pedantic King James!
To give us a "counter-blast" now in our times,
And help us to placard it everywhere
By all that is dear to us, "No smoking here!"

A DRINK OF MILK.

Come join me, of Temp'rance each Son and each Daughter,
   Teetotaler, Rechabite—a' o' that ilk;
Lang, lang hae we lilted the praise o' cold water,
   But now let us up wi' a bumper o' milk!

Say, what is ordained first for man as a bottle,
   When helpless he 's laid on a fond mither's lap?
Sure Nature designed him forever teetotal,
   In wisely providing then only—the pap!

Delightful 's the drink from the clear gushing fountain;
   Refreshing 's the draught from the clear gurgling rill
That flows down the glen or the side of the mountain;
   But strength'ning 's the willy-waught frae the milk-pail.

Baneful 's the drink from the vat of the vineyard;
   Madd'ning 's the dram from the barkeeper's jug;
Deadly 's the swill from the still of the swine-yard;
   But healthful 's the draught frae the dairy-maid's mug.

17

There are dogs, goats, and hogs, there are horses and asses,
  And likewise the sheep wi' the fleece yearly shorn,
But of a' the four-footed the hamestead possesses,
  There 's nane like the cow wi' the mild crookit horn.

Let friends who in kindness would treat us wi' dainties,
  Or high flavored drinks that our palates do please,
With curds and cream just frae the pantry present us
  Or wi' cakes butter-spread and a whang o' guid cheese.

O milk! everything both in palace and cottage!
  The choice of all tastes and of life the sweet stay!
A mercy the greatest from nonage to dotage!
  We hail thee, tho' drain'd of thy richness to whey!

Of the white fill the bowl, then, and let us be cheerie;
  Yes, every one o' us and each mither's bairn.
Down, down wi' distilleries and up wi' the dairy!
  Success to the milk-stoup, the cheese-vat, and kirn!

NANCY THE FAIR.

AIR: "ROBIN ADAIR."

Who was our village belle ?   Nancy, the fair !
Rich in accomplishments, quite debonair !
    Love's empire in her face—
    Her every movement grace—
    Nature's own masterpiece—
        'Bove all compare !

Many an honest swain called her his dear ;
But, of her charms elate, deaf was her ear.
    Praise bred conceit and pride.
    What ! she a peasant's bride !
    Such excellence must ride
        With titles rare !

What like her sliding heart should woman fear,
What—but the faithless rake, sly, insincere.
    Such ruined Nancy's name.
    Beauty's deceptive fame
    Gat her but guilt and shame
        Lastingly drear.

She, like a ghost forlorn, doomed to despair,
Now o'er her folly broods with bitter tear.
    Of peace and virtue shorn,
    Midst slighted lover's scorn,
    Fain would she cease to mourn,
        Stretched on her bier.

WEE PUSSIE'S ELEGY.

Away ye wha wi' hearts o' stane
Have never felt anither's pain,
But come ye that are pity's ain
      Wi' tears to shed,
And join me in my ruefu' strain—
      For Pussie dead.

Years hae elapsed—I think some twenty—
Sin' I received her frae my aunty,
Wow! then she was a kitten cantie
      As ever played
Wi' tail, in wheel-about-dance vaunty,
      Wee Pussie dead.

Whene'er I sat me down at leisure
Upon my knee she'd spring wi' pleasure,
And murr and thrum her sang's fond measure,
   Meanwhile her head
I wad hae stroked down to please her,
   My Pussie dead.

When I was at my porrich set,
Mewing, she wad hae trampt my fit,
And mensefu' for a soupie wait
   Wi' me to feed :
She never slunged the amury yet,
   Puir Pussie dead !

And when to bed we went to sleep,
She cozie at our feet wad creep,
Save when she took a hunting trip
   Under night's shade :
Nae mouse or rattan durst play cheep
   For Pussie dead.

Methinks I see her yet wi' grace
A-washing on the hud her face,
And scraping in the yard a place
   To do her need :
Nae sloven dirty marks ye 'd trace
   In Pussie dead.

When unco collie did intrude,
She 'd spit defiance and look wud,
Jumping a-four upon his fud
       Wi' claws o' dread :
Of dauntless heart and noble bluid
       Was Pussie dead.

When the corn-ricks were to take in
She was the foremost to begin ;
Soon as a mouse popped out to rin—
       'T was seized wi' speed ;
Now off they scamper wi' hale skin
       Since Pussie 's dead.

When Hallowe'en came wi' its " raid "
Nae witch on her yet rode astride ;
On sic nights o' infernal trade
       She kept her bed ;
Not void o' sense, tho' quadruped,
       ·Was Pussie dead.

Her coat-o'-fur was bottle-green,
The sleekest, prittiest e'er was seen;
Nane mair sae ever graced a queen
       As ruff when made ;
Now 't is the winding sheet, I ween,
       Of Pussie dead !

WILLIE DEER'S ELEGY.

A PET OF MISS SMAIL, OF KIRKMICHAEL MANSE, DUMFRIESSHIRE.

Come ye whase honest feeling heart,
Is touched at another's smart,
And in my wailing take a part
   Wi' pitying tear.
I 've lost, alack ! my darling hart,
   My Willie deer !

Where Kinnel in his winding gaiks
O'er shelving rocks, half-hid wi' aiks ;
Where woods of varied hue bedecks
   The landscape rare,
Was catched a caffie fu' o' freaks,
   My Willie deer !

At first he longed to be a-field,
At maiden kindness shy and wild,
But soon he tamed wi' treatment mild,
   And tender care ;
Like a beloved and only child
   Grew Willie deer.

O, Johnstone ! not a stagie spans
Wi' happier leap thy sylvan lawns,
Ev'n when the day delightfu' dawns
   In Summer cheer,
Than did a-sporting wi the fauns
   Here Willie deer.

When thro' the verdant fields I strayed
Across my path he skipping played ;
Or when I sat in bowery shade
   There was his lair :
A constant gay companion made
   My Willie deer.

Oft hae I stroked his glossy side
And flaunting gi'en him bits o' bread,
While his fond moppings me repaid.
   But now—nae mair—
Loathed and inactive wi' the dead,
   Lies Willie deer.

Nae huntsman's gun of thundering sound
Did lay him panting on the ground;
Nor did the fell-gore-greedy hound
          Ruthlessly tear;
Disease unknown, sly gave the wound
          Killed Willie deer.

Ah death! couldst thou not in yon grove
Where herds of deer unnumbered rove,
Glutted thy maw and scorned to move
          My fellow there?
Invidious wretch! to kill my love—
          My Willie deer.

I have a keepsake in his horn,
And (tho' the unfeeling laugh and scorn)
I to his memory at his urn
          A stone will rear,
To tell posterity unborn
          Thus Willie deer!

EPITAPH.

" The chiefest of the branching head!
The fleetest tenant of the glade!
The darling pet-hart of a maid
          Lies buried here!
Earth's dearest joys are a' but shade
          In Willie deer!"

BETHEL RELIEF SEWING SOCIETY.

Why flaps the Bethel flag to-day
  So joyous in the wintry blast?
Do pious sailors meet to pray,
  Give thanks, or hold a solemn fast?
The gangway 's open—let 's go in—
  O, what a scene is this we see!
The very pure and hallowed shrine
  Of Christian truth and charity.

The spacious cabin round and round
  Crowded with Cleveland's virtuous fair,
Joining the organ's lofty sound
  With voices charming, rich and rare?
No; all in order, graceful, still
  The needle and the shears they ply—
On cambric lace or silken frill?
  No; 't is the seam of charity.

Cooped in that nook a trio sit
  Of one thing-needful Marys, mild ;
And there 's a score of Marthas met
  Care-cumbered-much for orphan child.
On yonder side, with busy hand,
  Are Lydias, open-hearted, free;
On this an active Dorcas band,
  'Midst coats and cloaks of charity.

A faithful Eunice, here, the boys
  Tells of Timotheus' Bible fame ;
While there, a Ruth of noble choice
  Teaches the girls to sew the seam ;
A sprightly Rhoda at yon door
  Hails Jack, the wanderer of the sea,
To aid Salome for an hour
  In distributing charity.

To cut one little fellow's hair,
  And wash another's dirty face,
The helmsman for a while his care
  Foregoes, and rigs them up with grace.
And right—perhaps the same may shine
  As Newtons in philosophy,
As Judsons in the field divine,
  Or Howards yet in Charity.

*   *   *   *   *   *

Lo! what a freight, both fore and aft,
 Of infant mind—of rising youth!
If such of early culture 's 'reft,
 Oh! what will be the future growth!
For country! freedom! virtue! ruth!
 Come citizens, and helpers be,
To sow the seeds of sacred truth,
 And reap the fruits of charity.

There lay your treasure up in clothes—
 To the Great Giver are they lent;
Be sure they 'll not be eat with moths,
 And Heaven hath promised cent for cent.
For you—our city's diadem—
 Your sweet remembrance lasts for aye,
On orphan's cheek, the grateful gem
 Rewards your toils and charity.

RELIGIOUS POEMS

AND OCCASIONAL VERSES.

THE BIBLE A CLASS-BOOK.

———

Dear Bible classmates, as on past occasion,
Gladly I greet you at this celebration.
As a department of this Bethel School
'T is duty to conform to common rule;
To thus assemble with the rising youth,
Cheer on each other in the search of truth,
Join in one song, our varied corps review,
Recount our trophies and our toils renew!

The Bible—what a class-book we inherit!
Its author, God; indited by his Spirit.
Its grand design—to erring mortals given
To point the way and lead them up to heaven;
Old as creation, compassing all time,
Its truths affect eternity, sublime!

The Bible—what a class-book! every page
The masterpiece of the most learned Sage,

18

And yet so simply pleasing as to be
The school-boy's horn-book, or his A B C.
Do works historic, or the artistic page,
Travels, adventures, voyages engage?
Do things forensic, home or foreign news,
Theology or ethics most amuse?
Do strange events and truths of solemn weight,
· Sweet songs of joy, or sayings dark invite?
Does grand description, or the lofty ode
Hymning the work and wonders of a God?
Does narrative of friendship and of love
Delight the soul and most the passions move?
Well these and more we 've in this Book the best,
Suited to all of every caste and taste.

The Bible—what a class-book! to the full
As good for week day as for Sabbath School.
In simple diction or in classic style,
Here moral truths with heavenly graces smile.
Say not, an early or a common use,
Lessens esteem, or tends to an abuse,
Or that the Bible, thought to favor sect,
With secular studies should meet disrespect.

* * * * * * *

'T is flimsy all—nor merits a reply
To hearts that hark true wisdom from on high.

O, tell it not in Gath ! Our schools so famed
Without a Bible as a class-book named !

The Bible—what a class-book ! 't is a deed
Both signed and sealed by blood on Calvary shed;
That to the Christian in his wandering here
Is meat and drink—his counsel, stay, and cheer.
Of that blest land where mansions are prepared—
The map divine, and meets his whole regard ;
His compass on the stormy sea of life ;
His mighty sword, to conquer in the strife.

In every trial, every time of need,
The Sanctifier and the Friend indeed.
Yea more ; it furnishes his latest breath
With songs triumphant over sin and death,
Bestrews with flowers of heavenly balm the tomb,
And points beyond to scenes of endless bloom.

To this our class-book let us then take heed,
Like the Bereans, daily search and read ;
Like pious David, make both day and night
The law of God our study and delight ;
Like Abram, all obedient, believe ;
Like Jacob, pray, and blessing rich receive ;
Be meek like Moses, when tempted not o'ercome ;
Patient like Job, and meet bereavements dumb ;

Resolve, like Joshua, to serve the Lord;
Fear sin, like Joseph, and obtain reward;
Be strong, like Samson, and the foe subdue;
Devout, like Samuel, giving God his due;
Be like to Jonadab, for temperance famed;
And of our God, like Daniel, ne'er ashamed;
Blameless, like Zacharias, live in peace;
And waiting, like good Simeon, die in grace.

To be a Christian let us never wait—
Postpone like Felix to a time more fit;
Nor be like king Agrippa one almost,
Without a heavenly grace whereof to boast;
Nor like a worldly minded Demas, love
Secular emolument and recreant prove;
Nor turn blasphemous like the coppersmith,
Heart-hardened make sad shipwreck of the faith;
Nor once like Peter with an oath deny;
Nor with a traitor-kiss like Judas give the lie.

Hail highly honored women! unto you
In this our class-book are examples too.
With God's own people let your lot be cast,
Like loving Ruth, hence honored be at last;
If you would wed, for peace and comfort choose,
Like a Rebecca, a God fearing spouse;
Like Abigail, be prudent and discreet;
And like a Martha, on the table wait;

For public enterprise, a Dorcas prove;
And Lydia like, be rich in deeds of love;
Humble like Mary, choose the " better part "—
The one thing needful—"a renewed heart ";
And like a Eunice, train the raising youth
To know the Scriptures—feel their saving truth.
But above all, dear class-mates ! like to Christ
In all things may we be, and be divinely blest.

THE DYING WORDS OF JESUS.

Jesus, dear Saviour, Lord Divine !
Was love or pity e'er like thine ?
When ruthless ruffian soldier bands
Nail to the tree thy feet and hands,
'Midst mockery and torture great,
Without a murmur or a threat,
Thy prayer is for the murd'rous foe :
" Father, forgive ; they know not what they do."

Jesus, Messiah, Lord Divine !
Was ever saving work like thine ?
How great—tho' dying like a slave—
Thy willingness and power to save !
Let none presume, nor yet despond—
One dying thief repentance found !
At Jesus' word all sin 's forgiven—
" Verily to-day thou 'lt be with me in heaven."

Dear Babe of Bethlehem, Lord Divine!
Was filial duty e'er like thine?
Tho' racked with pain, and inly tried;
By friends betrayed, forsook, denied!
How for thy mother, standing near,
Pierced through with sorrows, thou dost care!
" Woman! behold in John thy son!
And now in mine, behold thy mother, John!"

Jesus, dear Saviour, Lord Divine!
Was ever anguish such as thine?
Suffering for sin the Father's wrath—
The hiding of his face in death—
The powers of hell and darkness nigh
Extort from thee, aloud, that cry
Of agony yet trust unshaken,
"My God! my God! how long by thee forsaken?"

Jesus, dear Saviour, Lord Divine!
Were ever sufferings such as thine?
The bloody sweat—the scourging borne—
The buffeting—the crown of thorn—
The travailing of soul—and loss
Of blood, long hanging on the cross,
As one by man, by God accurs'd,
Wrings from thy parched and fainting soul, " I thirst."

Jesus, dear Saviour, Lord Divine!
Was full redemption e'er like thine?
To mark thy mission at a close
With the completion of thy woes;
Type, promise, prophecy fulfilled;
Hell, death, the grave, and Satan que'led,
And heaven regained; with bowing head
Thou, conqueror, criest: "It is finished."

Jesus, dear Saviour, Lord Divine!
Was ever dying such as thine?
That Justice fully was appeased;
The Father with th' atonement pleased;
Thou freely death in mortal strife
Didst meet, the glorious Prince of Life!
Thy last are words of peace and merit,
"Father, into thy hand I yield my spirit."

BLIND BARTIMEUS.

PARAPHRASE ON MARK X: 46-52.

A. By the wayside blind Bartimeus
  Sat a-begging from his youth:
B. So by nature man the same is,
  Blind to every saving truth.

A. Hearing Jesus by was passing,
  ('T was the only time supposed;)
B. To secure the promised blessing
  Means appointed must be used.

A. " Pity, Lord, thou Son of David,"
  Was his persevering cry;
B. All by Jesus are relieved
  Who through faith to him apply.

A. Many bade him cease to trouble,
   But he cried the more in fear :
B. We should love the more our Bible—
   Bolder pray when scoffers sneer.

A. Christ stood still—thus called attention ;
   " Let the blind be brought to me."
B. Still he waits in condescension—
   Calls on all to " come and see."

A. " Rise ; he calls thee."   What a favor
   Falls upon the beggar's ear !
B. Those who see by faith the Saviour
   Will the darkling sinner cheer.

A. Throwing off his cloak and rising,
   Overjoyed he ran to Christ :
B. Stript of self, and sin despising,
   Converts, too, make gladsome haste.

A. " What wilt thou ?" inquired Jesus
   Kindly, " that I 'd do to thee ?"
B. Though he knows all our diseases,
   Yet inquired of he 'd be.

A. Earnestly the blind entreated,
   " Lord, my sight is what I crave !"
B. In the promise it is stated,
   Ask, if that ye would receive.

A.   "Go thy way, thy faith is saving,"
      Jesus said, and he was whole :
B.   Mercy honors the believing—
      Faith alone can save the soul.

A.   Now the man, midst light and beauty,
      Follows Jesus on the road :
B.   In the path of peace and duty
      The young Christian walks with God.

PARAPHRASE ON JOHN II:1, 2.

———

FOR THE SABBATH SCHOOL.

———

AIR: "*There's a friend that's ever near.*"

Children, while we learn of Jesus,
   While we offer praise and prayer,
Tell us why such duties please us,
   Or why God the same will hear?
We've the earnest of the Spirit
   In us in unspoken groan;
And the incense of the merit
   Of our great High Priest, God's Son!
     CHORUS—Let us never then despair,
         Fret or fear;
        He is ever there
         Ever us to cheer!

When our sin with heart contrition
  We confess, and pardon crave,
As a father in compassion
  He is ready to forgive.
Why ?—for penitent transgressor,
  Priest and Victim to atone,
We 've a mighty Intercessor
  In God's own accepted Son !
      CHO.—Let us never then despair.

Now no more the law we 're under,
  Or its blighting fatal curse :
All its charges spoke in thunder
  Lack condemnatory force.
Why !—its every one condition
  Hath been canceled—justice done,
By the great Propitiation
  Of the Father's righteous Son !
      CHO.—Let us never then despair.

Nothing present, nothing future,
  Plucks us from the Father's hand ;
Even Satan, the Disputer,
  Dare not harm us or withstand !
Why ?—we have become victorious—
  Death and Satan both o'erthrown,
Thro' our Head ascended glorious
  In our nature, God's dear Son !
      CHO.—Let us never then despair.

Yes, dear children! born to trouble,
  Sickness, trial, sin, and death;
Still, though all life's ills were double,
  We but suffer little scath.
Why?—we have with God the Father,
  All prevailing on his throne,
Both an advocate and brother
  In his well beloved Son!
    CHORUS—Let us never then despair,
           Fret, or fear;
          He is ever there
            Ever us to cheer.

IS MAN IMMORTAL?

———

Is man immortal?—Ask that feeble worm,
And it shall tell thee in its changing form:
To-day a larva crawling vile; the next
A chrysalis, as if in death transfixt;
Anon it bursts its cell, exultant, gay—
A butterfly, 'midst all the blaze of day!

Is man immortal?—Mark that little seed;
Dropt in the earth, awhile it lies as dead,
Till vernal showers descending on its tomb,
It springs to life and glorious spreads its bloom.

Is man immortal?—See! displayed abroad
The justice and the providence of God.
Sure vice not always shall escape the sword,
Nor suffering virtue lose the just reward.

Is man immortal?—If these proofs without
Fail to convince, look inward, and each doubt
Evanishes: His soul with powers so vast
And with desires so infinite, must last:

His horrors of nihility; his faith
In an existence lasting after death;
His act of thought, remaining unimpaired
Tho' in its every part the brain be marred;
His conscience, like a deity within,
Lauding the good, or damning what is sin;
His every passion—every faculty
Enstamps upon him: " Thou shalt never die !"

Is man immortal ?—Of the fact yet doubt ?
Then let the Gospel every scruple rout.
Incontrovertible, divinely bright,
There " immortality is brought to light."
Hope's anchor holding fast within the vail,
Tho' dangers, doubts, distress, and death assail,
While faith, rejoicing in the pleasant truth,
Anticipates the bliss of endless youth.

Yes; man 's immortal ! Scripture doth proclaim,
And nature's works, with reason, cry the same.

Hail, immortality ! and art thou mine,
With all thy greatness, all thy worth divine ?
Lord, grant me grace, on this infantine stage
To act--prepare for an eternal age,
When with new powers, along progression's road,
Near and more near I 'll 'proximate to God.

THE CHRISTIAN SOLDIER.

—

Hark! the gospel trumpet 's sounding!
   Bounty 's offered—peace and rest,
Grace to rebels still abounding.
   Come! whoever will, enlist
'Neath the glorious, all-victorious,
   Banner of the cross of Christ.

Marching through a hostile country
   Where temptations great assail,
Station at each sense a sentry,
   Lest such o'er the heart prevail;
Being strangers, placed midst dangers,
   Watchfulness will much avail.

Take the helmet of salvation,
   Gird on truth and righteousness;
Promised stores of ammunition
   Use, with prayer and every grace;
In the battle, strong and subtle,
   Yield to naught that mars thy peace.

19

See ! Messiah in his grandeur
  Conquering leads his chosen on ;
Having such a good commander,
  Rout or foul retreat there 's none.
Pressing onward in the vanguard
  Till the palm of victory 's won.

Shout the resurrection matin !
  Death, the grave, and hell despoiled,
At his chariot wheel is Satan
  Dragged in triumph—chained and foiled ;
While in heaven thrones are given
  Those who 'gainst him fought and toiled.

BE A CHRISTIAN.

Be a Christian ! what doth hinder?
  'Shamed of what some one may say ?
On the threat of Jesus ponder,
  Nor dare longer to delay.
"He that is of me ashamed
Shall in judgment be disclaimed."

Be a Christian ! a professor
  In the name of Christ your faith.
Be a Christian ! a possessor
  Of the purchase of his death—
Pardon, holiness, joy, peace,
Life eternal, every grace.

Be a Christian ! do earth's pleasures,
  Fame, or riches prove a snare ?
In religion there are treasures—
  Peace and joy not found elsewhere.
"What though all the world be gained,
When the soul 's lost in the end ?"

Be a Christian! do you stumble
　　At professors insincere?
Hypocrites indeed may tremble,
　　But the honest need not fear.
" Each one of himself must give
An account, and so receive."

Be a Christian! are you saying:
　　"At a more convenient time "?
Oh, the danger of delaying;
　　Death may overtake in crime!
" Boast not of to morrow's worth;
Who knows what a day brings forth ?"

Be a Christian! are you grieving
　　Over sins of such a hue
As can never be forgiven?
　　Read—the message is to you:
" Jesus' blood can from all sin
Wash the guilty conscience clean."

Be a Christian! think you merit
　　In one's self can save from sin?
Or that you without the Spirit
　　Through th' atonement heaven can win?
"Not by works; by grace we 're saved,
In the name of Christ believed."

Be a Christian ! are you doubting
   You 'll make shipwreck of the faith ?
Or in duties not hold out in—
   Fail to gain the prize at death ?
" His begun good work and true,
Shall be perfected in you."

Be a Christian ! do you waver ?
   'Fraid you will not be received ?
Firm the promise stands forever,
   Only let it be believed :
" Him that comes to me, no doubt—
I will in no-wise cast out !"

THE CHILD JESUS.

"And the child grew and waxed strong in spirit, filled with wisdom, and the grace of God was upon him."—LUKE ii : 40.

And was my Saviour, Jesus,
    A growing child like me ?
O, how the story pleases !
    Would like Him I could be !
Still waxing strong in spirit—
    With heavenly wisdom filled ;
Made, by His grace and merit,
    A humble, holy child.

How bright is the example !
    When at a tender age,
With teachers in the Temple,
    He shone the greater sage.
Be His my fixed endeavor—
    To do the Father's will ;
Found in His house forever ;
    Kept with His saints from ill.

He, subject to his mother,
　Still bids me mine obey;
While, being born a brother,
　His arm shall be my stay.
If He, the great Creator,
　Once earned his daily bread,
Shall I be 'shamed, the creature,
　To ply some honest trade?

The Babe of Bethlehem's manger,
　The youthful Nazarene,
Is no unfeeling stranger
　To childhood's lures to sin.
Restorer of man's nature,
　Immanuel! teach me,
While I increase in stature,
　To grow in grace—in Thee.

"KNOCK, AND IT SHALL BE OPENED UNTO YOU."

———

Knock! is the Gospel's special call,
Or invitation, free to all;
And this the promise kind and true—
" It shall be opened unto you."

Knock! how, or by what means, or where?
Admission only is by prayer;
And when the Father we implore
'T is through his Son—the way—the door.

Knock! at what time may this be done?
At morning, evening, and at noon—
At any hour; and we shall find,
To greet us there, a gracious Friend.

Knock! Holy Spirit, make this call
Effectual to each, to all;
Helping our failings by thy aid,
While we in prayer the promise plead.

Knock! but for what? First seek God's grace,
His kingdom and his righteousness;
Then all things temporal that we need
Shall richly be supplied indeed.

Knock! but how must we, to prevail?
With perseverance, faith, and zeal;
With patient waiting till he grant
His promised blessings—all we want.

Knock! not for aught in selfish greed;
Nor that of which we feel no need;
Nor what God has not said he'll give;
Nor when in wilful sin we live.

"ABBA FATHER."—A Prayer.

———

Abba Father! by creation
   I am thine, and would thee love;
Also thine by preservation,
   For in thee I live and move.

Abba Father! but by nature
  . Now the child of guilt and sin;
By thy Spirit a new creature
   Make me in Christ Jesus, clean.

Abba Father! I implore thee,
   Of thy family make me one;
Heir with Christ of God and glory—
   Of a bright, unfading crown.

Abba Father! me from folly,
   Vanity and vice preserve;
Never from thy precepts holy,
   Disobedient, let me swerve.

Abba Father ! I 've transgressed ;
  Yet be gracious—pardon me ;
Bless me and I shall be blessed—
  Ever living unto thee.

Abba Father ! in thy pity,
  Always in thy love correct ;
And in paths of peace and duty
  Gracious keep, and me direct.

Abba Father ! when affliction
  Come from thee, the righteous God,.
Let me not despise correction,
  But, submissive, kiss the rod.

Abba Father ! for thy tender
  Chastisements in love to me,
Ever grateful, will I render
  Homage, praise, and thanks to thee.

SHIP ZION.

———

Ho! the barge of King Immanuel
  Sails, as advertised, "to-day!"
Welcome all!—so reads the manual—
  All things ready, come away!
      Bound for glory,
      Trust the story,
  And in sin no longer stay.

Pilot at the helm is Jesus
  Who can bid the tempest cease;
Spirit's influence, the breezes,
  Fills the sails, the means of grace;
      While in honor
      Hoisted banner
  Waves—"The Lord our Righteousness."

Pious thoughts and duties holy
    Are the freight she 's bound to take;
Lest on reefs of sin and folly
    She should prove a fearful wreck,
        Ever prayerful,
        Watchful, careful,
    Conscience, watchman, walks the deck.

Chart and quadrant is the Bible;
    Faith the magnet, always true;
Each sure promise is the cable;
    Hope the anchor, fastened to
        God's eternal
        Throne supernal,
    Cheering ever on the crew.

For the peaceful port of Heaven,
    Come, then, every weary soul!
Free to all 's the transport given;
    Safe, tho' turgid waters roll.
        All on board now!
        Is the word now.
    Hark! and does the last bell toll?

WOMAN—THE TEMPORAL HEAD OF THE CHURCH.

Yes! in each age hath woman been
    The Church's best support and pride;
And so—in compliment, I ween—
    The Church is spoke of as a bride.
REVELATIONS xxi; EPHESIANS v.

When patriarch in her, as priest,
    Held friendly converse with her Head,
There was a Sarah to assist,
    And bake, for angel comers, bread.
GENESIS xviii.

Hers were a mother Jochebed,
    A sister Miriam, and the two,*
When she in Egypt groaned and bled—
    Drowning her sons because she grew.
EXODUS i: 15.

* Shiphrah and Puah.

When in the tented wild she lived,
  With skilful hand and willing heart,
Women for her stitched, spun, and weaved;
  Aye, with their jewels, too, did part.
                    EXODUS xxxv: 22-25.

When in the days of Judges' rule,
  Naomis, Hannahs, Ruths, Deborahs,
Did rule the work, the children school,
  And of her victories sing the chorus.
                    RUTH i—iv; JUDGES iv—v.

When in the times of kingly sway,
  To cheer 'mid trial and disaster,
She had an aunt Jehosheba,
  A noble Huldah, and Queen Esther.
                    ESTHER ix; II KINGS xxii: 14; xi: 2.

· And when her Husband, Lord, and King
  Awhile on earth incarnate tarries,
Were—of their substance ministering—
  Salome, Martha, and the Marys.
                    JOHN xi; MARK xv: 40.

Next, when the Apostles first did preach
  These Gospel truths now taught unto us,
She lacked not—both to serve and teach—
  A Dorcas, Lydia, Priscilla, Lois.
        ACTS ix: 36; xvi: 14; ROMANS xvi; II TIMOTHY i.

While many a one in heathen land
  Bow down to foolish god, or goddess,
For Jesus witnesses here stand,
  In sprightly Timothys and Rhodas.

ACTS xii: 13.

Then prized and praised be sister woman—
  " Mothers in Israel " is her story ;
In ages past, in ages coming,
  The Church's bulwark, hope, and glory.

THE SOLDIERS' AID FAIR.

——

Give it up ?—Yes, Jeff Davis may now give it up !
   Each slaveholder die in despair !
At sight of our " troops of reserve " there 's no hope.
   Hurra ! for the Soldiers' Aid Fair.

Whatever is rare both in nature and art,
   Things novel and ancient are here—
Inventions of past, and of future desert,
   Are all at the Soldiers' Aid Fair.

But what is there not here all praise to command,
   Tho' vain the attempt to declare ?
The beautiful, useful, amusing, and grand,
   Are all at the Soldiers' Aid Fair.

Be enrich'd with the sight, then, good citizens all ;
   Such a chance in a lifetime is rare.
Our country now claims it ; and then there 's the call
   Of those *dears* of the Soldiers' Aid Fair.

20

Ye brave Union heroes! march on in your fame;
  'T is you, in the right, that can dare,
Whose mothers, wives, sisters, and sweethearts acclaim
  By their deeds, thus at the Soldiers' Aid Fair.

Was London's glass palace—a whole world's resort—
  More splendid than this on our Square?
Pshaw! one little State can arise in her sport
  And match it in Soldiers' Aid Fair.

Not Egypt, slave-chasing, was terror-struck more
  By the pillar of fire's red glare,
Than Southern rebellion o'erwhelmed in its power
  By the rod of our Soldiers' Aid Fair!

AT THE FIRST DECORATION OF SOLDIERS'
GRAVES, MAY, 1869.

——

Come, let us bring the choicest flowers of spring
  And decorate the patriot soldier's grave.
Would that the humble yearly offering
  Might tell of their achievements vast and brave,
And that their memories, ever, ever dear,
Are hallowed by a nation's grateful tear.

Here, let affection's sweetest flowers be piled—
  The husband kind and honored father sleep.
Behold! the faithful wife and loving child,
  Both inconsolable and kneeling weep.
It was not theirs on carnage battle-grounds
  To share his toils, or bind his bleeding wounds.

Yon grave with modest violets let be clothed—
  There a meek maid demurely mourneth one.
Senseless beneath the turf, her dear betrothed
  In death's long-locked embrace hears not her moan.
Love's token sent, doth on her finger tell
His last faint breathings, " Lucy, fare thee well."

Upon *that* tomb let roses scent the breeze—
  See! a lone widow mourns her only boy.
He was her sole support, but drums did please,
  And martial fame waked aspirations high.
Famished in prisons, he returned—alas!
Only to die, and find a resting place.

Yes; drop a bouquet on the alien's grave.
  'Midst Freedom's serried ranks he fighting fell.
Not for his country did he dangers brave;
  Nor was it that he might secession quell.
For God and right—to crush tyrannic lord
And free the oppressed flamed his avenging sword.

Strew fairest blossoms on *that* sacred mound.
  An angel heroine reclines beneath.
'T was hers by day, by night, to dress the wound
  Of friend, of foe, and cheer the soul in death.
Endeared to thousands, overdone she lies,
To broad humanity a sacrifice!

Ruler o'er all—our Pilgrim fathers' God!
  We own thy dealings mercifully just.
Thou wrought'st deliverance; we kiss the rod
  And in the future on thine arm would trust.
Let unity and peace flow like a river,
To bless our nation, henceforth, even forever.

HELP THE ORPHANS.

———

AN APPEAL AT A ST. ANDREW'S FESTIVAL.

———

Come ye wha wad honor the saint o' the Scot,
And gie to our Orphan Asylum a groat.
True charity never takes time to discern
Whether Yankee or Scotch be the fatherless bairn.

A shake-down o' straw, and an amery toom;
Nae ingle nor candle, to banish the gloom;
While Winter drifts in thro' the chinky wa's stern;
O! wha wadna' pity the mitherless bairn.

The puir wee bit lassie, wi' weather-bleached hair;
The puir wee bit laddie, feet hackit and bare,
A' duddy and dirty, begruthen, forfairn;
O, wha wadna' pity the fatherless bairn!

'T is hard to encounter the sleet and the snaw,
Baith hungry and sarkless, bare-headed and a'!
And harder to brook still the pampered fop's spurn;
O, wha wadna' pity the fatherless bairn!

O grudge not, nor deem what you gie will be vain!
You lend to the Lord, wha returns a' wi' gain!
These objects may thraw yet a stane to your cairn—
May bliss in their turn, yours, the fatherless bairn!

THE ORPHANS' BAZAAR.

AIR—"BUY A BROOM,"

Kind friends, come and buy of us some little notion;
   Our nations of rarities are at your choice.
The cause of the orphan must have your devotion,
   While young ones at home in your gifts will rejoice.
      Buy our toys, buy our toys,
   That orphans and loved ones at home may rejoice.

Here 's books, see! the drollest, to study at leisure;
   And pictures at which you may laugh yourselves fat;
Here 's sweetmeats and candies, if such be your pleasure,
   In form of the elephant, horse, dog, or cat.
      Buy a cat, buy a cat;
   Of creatures domestic there 's none like the cat.

Here 's articles both ornamental and useful,
 And cheap, that we fear you will think they were stole.
O ! surely you 've not got at home such a houseful
 But that there 's a place for this fine little doll.
   Buy a doll, buy a doll,
 Dear Jeannie expects you to buy her a doll.

O pity the orphan ! no father nor mother
 Has he to get for him what's needful to life ;
While your little fellows, all playful together,
 Proudly boast of their sled, of their skates, of their knife.
   Buy a knife, buy a knife,
 That the orphan may get what is needful for life.

Yes ; give to the orphans—the children of Heaven—
 He will in return " bless your basket and store."
Give freely—not grudgingly let aught be given ;
 Your dear ones may lack yet the mite we implore.
   We implore, we implore,
 That Heaven may bless both your basket and store.

UPON THE DEATH OF MRS. PROSSER.

—

Her place is vacant round the hearth—
No more her sweet domestic worth
   The family circle cheers.
Gone to a mansion in the sky,
Where home endearments never die,
   She knows no grief nor cares.

Then let not sorrow's hopeless tear
Be shed by child or husband dear;
   A few short years, and then,
In a society more blessed—
Their Father, God; their Brother, Christ;
   They all shall meet again.

Her place within the house of God—
Oh! how the sailors feel the void—
   On willows hang their lyre.
No more in Bethel songs her voice
Seraphic leads the "joyful noise,"
   And swells the general choir.

But why repine ?   Now, with the throng
Of the redeemed, she sings the song
   Of Moses and the Lamb.
'Mong all the host of worshipers,
No higher note of praise than hers,
   Or love of purer flame.

Ye children of the Sabbath School—
With grief your hearts and eyes are full;
   Beloved Teacher gone !
The pious precepts she did teach,
O let your future conduct preach—
   Be her memorial stone.

Ye Bible-class mates—most of all,
To you is made this solemn call.
   The first upon our list,
Active and most esteemed, is gone.
Who of us next will be the one
   That joins her in "that rest" ?

Divine Instructor! grace afford,
That we may love, like her, Thy Word,
   And dying tell its joys—
When faith is changed to open vision,
And prayer and hope to blest fruition,
   Immortal in the skies.

ON THE DEATH OF C—— G——.

A SABBATH SCHOOL SCHOLAR, FIRST PRESBYTERIAN CHURCH,
CLEVELAND, KILLED BY THE CARS.

AIR—*"Long, long ago."*

Vacant 's a seat in our school-room to-day ;
    Charlie is gone ; ever gone !
Silent the voice that once joined in our lay ;
    Charlie is gone ; ever gone !
Suddenly snatched from our Sabbath School here
Up to an heavenly—friends yet more dear—
Bible truths taught him, now perfectly clear.
    Charlie is gone ; ever gone !

Loud, as in thunder, the accident cries :
    Charlie is gone ; ever gone !
"Watch and be ready—who next of us dies ?"
    Charlie is gone ; ever gone !
Over him rushes the merciless train ;
Crushed like a flower, has he budded in vain ?
Brighter in glory he blossoms again,
    Charlie that 's gone ; no, not gone.

With his lone parents we drop sorrow's tear;
    Charlie is gone; ever gone!
He was a hopeful son, only and dear,
    Charlie that 's gone; ever gone!
Taken away from the evil to come,
Happy in youth's incorruptible bloom,
Ministrant angel, he beckons them home,
    Charlie that 's gone, no, not gone!

Yet a short while, and we all too must leave,
    Charlie like, gone; ever gone!
Of all our Sabbaths account full to give,
    Charlie like, gone; ever gone!
O, may it be to receive the proud palm—
Wave it triumphant and join in the psalm
Of all the ransomed ones—" Worthy the Lamb,"
    With Charlie gone; no, not gone!

ON W—— P——.

A Boy about Ten Years Old, Drowned while bathing in the Cuyahoga River, July 1, 1862.

In the dark Cuyahoga river,
  Willie with his playmates lave—
Life 's uncertain, death is never—
  Willie sinks beneath the wave.
    Mourn him, ye his comrades all;
    Are you ready should death call?

Faithful, loving, and engaging—
  Never stubborn, seldom wrong—
In his manner so obliging,
  He was loved by old and young.
    Mourn him, ye whose daily toils
    Oft were sweetened with his smiles.

Better culture and example
  Lacked he for his sudden change?
Speaks the event of blessings ample,
  Chastisements or judgments strange?
    Mourn him, parents—kiss the rod,
    And train your children up for God.

Sabbath and its school returning,
  Was to him the best of days—
Happiest while of Jesus learning,
  And in chanting forth his praise.
    Mourn him, classmates, now as one
    Of the ransomed 'round the throne.

BETHEL SABBATH SCHOOL.

What is this our eyes behold ?—
Kings and courtiers decked in gold ?
Armies for the carnage bold ?
       No,—the Sabbath School.
Met beneath the mystic Dove,
Children chant their songs of love
Like the seraph host above,
       Sweet and beautiful.

Happy scene, and blest, forsooth !
Churches throng'd with rising youth,
Come to learn the way of Truth—
       Wisdom's early choice.
O ! ye loved ones ! active, gay,
Now 's the spring-tide of your day.
Sow the seed that reap you may
       Never-fading joys.

Mark with gratitude the zeal,
Manifested in your weal.
Let your future conduct tell
       Sabbath lessons given.
Parents! send your children here;
Christ, to bless, invites them near.
Come yourselves; what if their cheer
       Leads you, too, to heaven?

Patrons! Teachers! cheerily toil;
Sion's King our foes shall foil;
Vast will be the Victor's spoil;
       Forward—let us press!
See! the nations tremble, all.
Satan's vanquished of his thrall.
Hark! great Babel in her fall
       Cries, alas! alas!

God of Bethel! whose right hand
Led our fathers to this land,
Promised blessings still command
       Here on us their seed.
Raiment fit and food provide;
Be our portion, God, and Guide,
Let thy house be verified
       Heaven's gate indeed!

CHURCH DEDICATION.

———

God the Father, Son, and Spirit,
  In thy sacred name we meet—
Taking to ourselves no merit—
  Now this house to dedicate
To thy holy service wholly :
  Deign thyself to consecrate !

When immensity so ample
  With thy might and goodness swell,
When eternity thy temple
  Half thy praises cannot tell,
What 's this house then to thy use then ?
  Yet with contrite hearts thou 'lt dwell.

Of thy bounty freely given
  Back again receive a part.
Now by grace redeemed for heaven
  Thine we are and ours thou art.
In this union and communion
  Take this offering of our heart.

Let thy footsteps here be glorious—
  Beautiful in holiness.
Lead thy people on victorious
  In thy saving power and grace.
Like the adorning dews of morning
  Let true converts throng this place.

When to thee is made petition
  From this place, O ! lend an ear;
And when thou behold'st contrition,
  Pity, save, and whisper cheer—
All things granting that 's awanting
  To advance thy kingdom here.

Lord, may never passions hateful
  Peace destroy or faith disprove ;
But with hearts and voices grateful
  Let our songs be blent in love :
To each other acting brother
  Till we meet in bliss above.

JEHOVAH, OR GOD'S MEMORIAL NAME.

———

Say, what is God's memorial name,
To generations all "the same,"
    Even to eternity ?
Jehovah! of His word the scope,
Of every promise there the hope,
    "I 'll be who I will be."

        Exodus iii : 14, and xxiii : 21.

But of what import unto me,
The child of sin and misery,
    Is this peculiar word ?
Jehovah Jesu ! He who can
Only redeem lost, ruined man—
    His " Saviour, Christ the Lord."

        Matt. i : 21 ; Luke ii ; 11.

Guilty and all diseased by sin,
No soundness found without, within—
    Can there be hope for me ?
Jehovah rophi ! At his word
Life, health, joy, peace, all are restored
    " By him who healeth thee."

        Exodus xv : 26 ; Hosea vi : 1, 3.

A wanderer poor, from home afar,
With wretched self and God at war,
  Have I his special care ?
Jehovah shammah ! He is nigh—
Thy Shepherd, shield, and tower high,—
  Thy " name, I will be there."
     EZEKIEL xlviii : 35 ; DANIEL iii : 25.

But what should joys and comforts fail ;
Wants, straits, and trials hard assail—
  Perplexed on every side ?
Jehovah jireh !   On him lean
At all times, and it shall be seen,
  " He will be to provide."
     GEN. xxii : 14 ; DANIEL 2.

A friendless exile, in whose path
Lie hidden dangers, snares, and death—
  In whom can I confide ?
Jehovah allooph !   With his staff,
His rod and conusel you can laugh
  In safety, " He 's your guide."
     PSALMS lxxiii : 24 ; JEREMIAH iii : 4.

But doubts and fears distract the soul,
And passions rage beyond control,
  With conscience ill at ease.
Jehovah shalom !   Joyous rest
He 'll give the weary, troubled breast,
  Yea " will be thy sent peace."
     JUDGES vi : 24 ; MATT. xi : 28.

How can I quell my wicked heart—
Foil Satan's every fiery dart,
    And triumph o'er the grave ?
Jehovah nissi!   In the fight
Thou 'rt more than conqueror in his might ;
    " He will thy banner wave."
           EXODUS xvii : 15 ; ROMANS viii : 37.

Beset with hosts of subtile foes,
Which flesh and blood cannot oppose :
    Ah ! whither shall I flee ?
Jehovah sabaoth !   Up ! be brave !
Thy Captain, mighty, comes to save,
    " The Lord of armies, He ! "
           JOSHUA v : 14 ; ROMANS ix : 29.

The promise of his coming where ?—
All things continue as they were ?
    What signs doth one descry ?
Jehovah Elyion !   King of heaven !
To whom earth's kingdoms all are given,
    The Christ—even " God most high."
           PSALMS ii : 7 ; REV. xi : 15.

Mysterious ! aye, the " coming one,"
" The Almighty God, yet very man,
    Of universal rule ! "
Jehovah pelai !   The I Am !
In person, office, work, and name,
    Divinely " wonderful ! "
           JUD. xiii : 18 ; COL. 1 : 18, 19.

On what foundation can I place
My hopes of future happiness,
    And feel that I 'm secure ?
Jehovah tsur olamim ! Known
As Sion's living corner-stone,
    " The Rock of Ages, sure ! "
                ISAIAH xxvi : 4 ; MATT. vii : 25.

A broken law, and still in force—
Am I condemned to bear its curse ;
    Where is my subterfuge ?
Jehovah shophetnu ! The end
Of that same law, thy brother, friend,
    Thy advocate, " thy Judge ! "
                ISAIAH xxiii : 22 ; I JOHN ii : r.

Devoid of merit, can I claim
The blessings of this gracious name,
    So suited to my case ?
Jehovah tsedek ! all we want
Is he our kinsman, pledged to grant,
    " The Lord our righteousness."
                JER. xxiii : 6 ; I COR. i : 30.

Be, then, hosannas to his name,
Who is, was, and to come the same—
    The world's deliverer !
Jehovah malak ! From man's fall
Till restitution, all in all !
    " The Covenant's Messenger ! "
    MAL. iii : 1 ; REV. i : 8 ; HEB. xiii : 8 ; COL. iii : 11.

CPSIA information can be obtained
at www.ICGtesting.com
Printed in the USA
BVHW030915020119
536754BV00009B/5/P

9 781165 212880